the SECRET DIARY
of **BILL GATES**

the SECRET DIARY* of BILL GATES

A PARODY

"Bill G."

Andrews McMeel Publishing

Kansas City

www.andrewsmcmeel.com

98 99 00 01 EBI 10 9 8 7 6 5 4 3 2 1

Library of Congress Cataloging-in-Publication Data

G., Bill.
    The secret diary of Bill Gates : a parody / Bill G.
        p.   cm.
    Includes bibliographical references (p.).
    ISBN 0-8362-5204-7 (pbk.)
        1. Gates, Bill, 1955– —Humor. 2. Computer software industry—United States—Humor. 3. Businessmen—United States—Humor. 4. Microsoft Corporation—Humor.
    I. Title.
    HD9696.C62G335   1998
    818'.5407—dc21   97-49897
                                        CIP

Design by Lee Fukui

CONTENTS

ACKNOWLEDGMENTS

This book is based on my awesome Web site, "The Secret Diary of Bill Gates"—the #1 most popular site on the Net about you-know-who! (Apart from the "official" Microsoft site, of course.) Over one million hits a month as the world's Bill-a-holics get their latest fix! Check out the latest moves and grooves in my life at:

http://www.billg.org

Special thanks to: my Net babes Elwira, Jennifer, Krista, Maya, Melinda, and Nina. Yeaahhh! Thanks to Nagai-san my Japan partner, funky SimonR, MikeW, Kate my abfab agent, and MattL my way cool editor at Andrews McMeel. And everyone who writes to me! And my mom and dad!

DISCLAIMER

Look it's a joke, OK? A PARODY.

A work of fiction, for entertainment purposes only. Any reference to real people (living or dead) or their e-mail correspondence, actual locales, historical events, stock trading, or computer products are used solely to lend the fiction an appropriate cultural, historical, and technological setting. All other names, characters, places, and incidents portrayed here are the product of the author's imagination, and any resemblance to actual persons, living, dead, or in cryogenic suspension, is entirely coincidental.

I'm not Bill Gates, I'm not in charge of Microsoft, and I don't have any money. (The World's Richest Man is writing his diary and talking to the little people via e-mail? Give me a break!) I don't have a clue about Bill, Melinda, and Jennifer's private life. I'm making this up. As far as I know, they are warm, caring, and utterly wonderful people. (As, of course, are Steve Jobs, Larry Ellison, Marc Andreessen, Scott McNealy, and everyone at the DoJ.) I'm sure they can see the funny side of my little work of authorship!

Bill Gates is great. He rules! He's done a fantastic job in building Microsoft to the preeminent position it holds today, and he deserves every cent of his obscenely large fortune.

Sincerely,

Bill G. (but not Bill Gates, OK?)

P.S.: This is purely a personal work, and in no way connected with, or representative of, Bill Gates or Microsoft. Thanks to everyone for their contributions to the Diary. Enjoy!

the SECRET DIARY of **BILL GATES**

Oh, boy. Life sure is tough as the go-getting CEO of Microsoft—the megacorporation heading for global computer and technology domination. All those employees, meetings, and important people to talk to. But it's worth it: we're the world's best-loved software corporation. (We must be—we're the biggest!) Then there's the Internet. It's cool. It's not Word or Excel, of course, but it's still pretty significant. Things are happening so fast, I have to really concentrate. Otherwise, I might get left behind by those losers over at Netscape, Oracle, and Sun.

On the domestic front, there's my new waterfront techno-palace (not just cool, but fifty million dollars of cool!) and choosing the appropriate Corbis art and ambient sounds for those wall-sized video screens. Juggling my new family commitments as Melinda's superstud and rich Daddy to my supersmart Baby Jennifer. And, of course, my fitness campaign. Busy, busy, busy...

These are significant changes in my life, and I'm feeling somehow more introspective. Those twenty Microsoft years have just flown by! And the forties and fatherhood are major guy milestones: they change your perspective on life, and suddenly, where you're getting your next billion dollars from doesn't seem so important.

That's why I decided to keep my Secret Diary—so Jennifer can read it someday and see that I'm not just any old billionaire daddy, I'm also a supercool guy. (And the richest billionaire daddy around!)

Then some loser hacked his way into the Diary files and started publishing them on the Internet. So much for the "Secret" part, huh? But then I thought, maybe I am being just a little selfish. Maybe the world should have the benefit of my most private thoughts. (Sometimes charity goes beyond dollars and cents, Ted. But you wouldn't understand.)

So, here it is! What a great follow-up to my worldwide #1 hit, *The Road Ahead*. Enjoy! And remember, don't be selfish—buy copies for all of your friends!

Sincerely,

Bill G. :-)

"The unfolding year reveals the pattern of our true and secret lives." ADRIAN MOLE

WEDNESDAY, JANUARY 1

NEW YEAR'S DAY—NATIONAL HOLIDAY, EVEN AT MICROSOFT

Happy New Year, Microserfs! The harbinger of the infosphere returns. Another year, another billion dollars...

Just got back from Palm Springs. It's nice, but way too warm. I think I prefer plenty of rain. On the other hand, there's nothing like a couple of days of golf to get me relaxed and ready to face another year of competitor crushing. (It gets my competitive juices flowing.)

Here are my New Year's resolutions:

Resolution #1 (no, nothing to do with competitor crushing): Improve my golf game. I'm hardcore about achieving a significant (year on year) reduction of my handicap. I mean, hey, what's the point of playing unless you can win?

Resolution #2: Crush Netscape. (OK, I couldn't resist.)

Resolution #3: Keep a diary! It'll be tough to fit diary writing into my hectic schedule, but I'll get one of the boys to ghostwrite the first draft.

3

Myhrvold, my loyal lieutenant, thinks he's John Grisham since making his epic contribution to my worldwide best-seller, *The Road Ahead*. (Buy it, OK?) I'll pencil him in for diary duties...

It's a week since Christmas, and Melinda still hasn't tried on that underwear from Victoria's Secret that I bought her. It looked pretty good in their catalog. Perhaps she would have preferred a copy of new Microsoft Office?

THURSDAY, JANUARY 2

It's officially back to work here at Microsoft. I just don't believe that some of these guys actually took yesterday off—don't they understand the work ethic? And worse, they're still not fully functioning units: more Hangover City than Microsoft Campus. The number of brain cells that died, pickled in alcohol, this weekend! I figure there's a bunch of developers who are now sliding desperately down the wrong side of that bell curve to the 150s. Ha! Eat my dust, guys! But, seriously, I wouldn't be where I am today without their help, which I TRULY appreciate. (Just practicing for my next talk show!)

And Apple buys NeXT for $400 million and the next MacOS will be based on the NeXT OS. (Get it? I'm such a funny guy!) This deal brings Steve Jobs (industry golden boy and "talented visionary") back to the company he founded twenty years ago as "adviser to the Chairman/CEO." Made-up job title alert!

Anyway, it's too late to save Apple now (unless I step in and help them): their SEC filing paints a dismal picture, with a Q4 market-share drop to 5.4% worldwide. The lack of demand for Apple product "was due principally to customer concerns regarding [Apple's] strategic direction, financial condition, and future prospects," the filing said. Right. That and they're total losers...

Resolution #4: Read again, and finally understand, the quantum theory of gravity. Nathan says it's easy, but he'll explain the math for me if I still have problems...I hate Nathan.

FRIDAY, JANUARY 3

ADMISSION DAY (ALASKA)

I **know** the New Year is the time for resolutions, but it's also a good time to go out on a limb and make radical predictions for the next twelve months. This will demonstrate my ability as an industry VISIONARY and prognosticator (another good word, huh?). So here are my New Year's Predictions:

1. I'll make the cover of *Time,* at least once. (And *Wired* too, but who cares about them?)

2. The stock price of Microsoft (MSFT) will hit $150 per share. (This is a self-interested prediction, since I hold a whole bunch of Microsoft stock, but I think it's absolutely

true. Actually, as it takes my net worth close to $50 billion, I guess it's a VERY self-interested prediction. Ha, ha.)

3. The Internet will be even bigger this year than last year. In fact, it will be really, really big. (In retrospect, committing to the Internet seems so obvious that now it's hard to keep a straight face.)

4. Most corporations will employ electronic mail systems by the end of the year, and employees will typically send or receive e-mail several times a day. (I really went WAY out on that limb for this one. A truly fearless prediction.)

5. Sometime this year my house will get FINISHED. (Are you paying attention, construction guys? What's your industry equivalent of "vaporware"?)

SATURDAY, JANUARY 4

Into orbit! Picked up a copy of *Time* at Barnes & Noble, and guess what? I'm on the cover! (And with my new, rounded glasses that Melinda picked out for me recently for that "hip, older dude in an Eric Clapton kind of way" look. And they were clean, too!) I'm just so cool! And one of my predictions is true already! I AM a visionary! (Sometimes I'm so right, it's scary.)

Although I do have to say that it's slightly disappointing as I was expecting to be their Man of the Year. I mean, everybody's heard of me. But Dr. David Ho? I don't think so. It's just so frustrating. A few years back, they just wanted to talk about Jobs and Kahn and Manzi and other "industry VISIONARIES." Now it's AIDS researchers as modern idols. I just don't get it. Still, "the world's most famous businessman and also its richest person." I guess that'll have to do...

Resolution #5: Stop watching the Microsoft stock price so much. (Hey, it's only money. And I long ago overtook the Sultan of Brunei...Old "Tea-Towel Head" has been "sheik-en" from the top spot. Ha, ha.)

SUNDAY, JANUARY 5

Actually, I e-mailed that *Time* guy, Walter Isaacson, about that intro. I'm NOT a businessman. I'm a technologist. A whiz kid. A VISIONARY. Businessmen are so boring. Who wants to be a businessman? I certainly don't. I wanted to be a scientist. Or a mathematician. I wanted to win the Nobel Prize. (What businessman ever won it, huh?) Still, I won't get much response from him. He's one of those touchy-feely guys who wants to discuss "personal philosophy" and other mushy stuff. Mainly because he's not sharp enough to discuss real, hardcore technical issues. Still, I must admit it was pretty entertaining when I drove him around to see my house. It's nearly midnight, it's raining, and I'm racing around in my Lexus. He can't figure out whether to put his seat belt on. So I look at him, rather than the road (boy, that always freaks them out!) and put my foot down. The guy is nearly wetting himself... Calm down, Walter, it's just a car ride! Loser!

Resolution #6: Don't get any more speeding tickets!

Resolution #7: Update my wardrobe at the January sales. And save money! What a thrifty guy I am...

"Mirror, mirror, on the wall, who is the smartest of them all?" BILL G.

MONDAY, JANUARY 6

This really is the last time I relax over the Christmas holiday. In the future, Kristi and Libby can get in line with everyone else and just send me e-mail!

Today, I'm at breakfast with Melinda, and I'm doing my rocking backward and forward thing. Trying to intimidate her into seeing things my way. It doesn't work, of course, and she orders me to sit still for a few minutes. And that's when the realization hits me...I CAN'T stop. My body is this disconnected object that won't respond to my (object-oriented) commands. Like I'm using IBM 3270 protocol to communicate with a typewriter. So, this brings me to...

Resolution #8: Subjugate my body. I've lived in the playground of the mind too long. I mean, I know I'm a good looking guy and all, but I've never really made the effort to, like, tone my body. This could be the year of the buff Bill bod. Ha, ha.

I tell Melinda I'm going to my bedroom. And I check out the push-up situation. Is four any good? I'm guessing here, but I suspect I'm not quite ready for *American Gladiators*. But, hey, Microsoft wasn't built in a day...

TUESDAY, JANUARY 7

Surfing the wave of my incredible early success with my New Year's predictions, I've come up with a few more. (Remember: I'm going out on a limb here in my continuing efforts to demonstrate my industry-visionary-ness.) So here are the others:

6. A large fraction of the U.S. public will have made purchases on the Net by the end of the year. Secure Internet transactions will transform the commercial value of the Internet

and we'll be happy to give our VISA numbers on-line. (I guess this means I'll have to stop using Melinda's credit card for on-line transactions at Ben & Jerry's and Amazon.com and start using my own. Bummer!)

7. Digital video disks (DVDs), with twenty times more data capacity than their CD-ROM predecessors, will become the major new standard this year, with broad PC support. The simple concept of putting a complete movie on a CD will begin the unification of the living room home entertainment system with the office PC. (This is a self-interested prediction, as Microsoft is investing heavily in this area, but I think it's absolutely true.)

8. Hard though it may be to believe (trust me, I'm the VISIONARY), handheld PCs will grow in popularity by more than, hmmmm, 50%. That's at least another 500,000 in use by the end of the year. Within a few years, these wallet PCs will be more popular than cell phones are today. (Of course, this is another self-interested prediction, as guess what they'll be running? How about Windows CE? Way coooool!)

9. Advertising revenue on the Internet will soar. (This is another self-interested prediction, as I'm selling ad space on my Secret Diary Web site, but I think it's absolutely true. You can see the ads already!)

10. Sometime later in the year, Jennifer will speak her first full sentence: "That's the stupidest thing I've ever heard, da-da." (Again, this is a self-interested prediction, as I'm her pop, but I think it's absolutely true. Unless it's "ma-ma.")

WEDNESDAY, JANUARY 8

Got a press release from myself this morning.

It's always great to know what we've been doing. Apparently, last year, we invested in, or acquired, over twenty companies and spent nearly $1 billion. In comparison, those losers down at Netscape only managed a miserable eight acquisitions. I should keep a more careful eye on things, though. We went and bought 5% of WebTV Networks. We wouldn't have made such a heavy investment if I'd known. (That must have been Nathan "We're a Content Company Now" Myhrvold.)

Some of my other resolutions are:

Resolution #9: Get *Slate* a complete makeover. (Compost!) What's wrong with pictures of naked chicks, rock 'n' roll, and video-game reviews... and a Gillian Anderson interview?

Resolution #10: Be less competitive.

Resolution #11: Crush Novell! (Oops. Did that last year.)

And what about MacWorld? Or the new

Macintosh Product Unit? Really, what's the point? Looks like all the work we did on IE for the Mac was a big waste of time. (Although I guess the Mac Product Unit goes a long way toward convincing Apple that an IE bundling deal is a brilliant idea!) But a great quote from Steve Jobs at the show...He's claiming that the key to Apple's success in the future is to deliver "relevant, compelling solutions." I'd worry if I didn't have twenty years of experience that proves that Apple only ever delivers solutions that are compelling or relevant to Californians on drugs!

Final resolutions:

Resolution #12: Be kinder to people less intelligent than myself. (There are plenty of them. Ha, ha.)

Resolution #13: Be kinder to people poorer than myself. (Lord knows there are even more of THEM.)

Melinda says that she saw me doing my push-up the other day. She says it was a most excellent push-up, perfect in both form and function, but that a few more are usually required for beneficial cardiovascular and muscular results.

I don't understand it! All this rubbish that's been written about Steve Jobs this week...Stuff like "How many other companies with a 5% market share have a leader (or 'adviser to the Chairman/CEO') who generates so much press?" I generate more press in the average month than he's done, ever! AND I've got the other 95% market share, thank you very much.

Called a meeting with our Human Resources people. I'm totally determined to remove all Buzz Lightyear figures from the workplace. And anyone I catch shouting "To infinity...and beyond!" loses all his stock options.

Bad news on the Melinda front. Apparently, I suffered a catastrophic memory crash last week. I didn't remember our anniversary. (How could I forget January 1, 1994, in Hawaii? Sand, sea, sun, and...) Now, I may have to buy her a small present. Like Brazil.

She says if we're not going anywhere, can we go out to dinner tonight? She wants to go to Myhrvold's hobby, one of Seattle's leading French restaurants. I've seen his software, why would I want to risk his cooking?

I took a look at MSN's Mungo Park...Way cool!
Looks like Laura Jennings is doing something right!
Maybe hiring all these women will have some bene-
fits other than just making Microsoft look like an
equal-opportunity employer...

SUNDAY, JANUARY 12

Now imagine the music of the future...
There'd be no need to worry about what artists you
like/dislike...no borrowing new CDs from guys in
the office to check out if they're worth taping, er, I
mean buying. Just choose the style of music you'd
like to listen to (Memphis Blues, Rock Ballads, or
Debussy-style), choose how you want it played
(acoustic, electric, or synthesized), and simply click
the mouse! Beautiful music floods from your PC
speakers, generated on the fly, for your ears only.
Pretty cool, huh? An impossible dream? Wrong! Get
over to my main site and download new Microsoft
Music Producer. It's the future of music, today!
(Another blatant Microsoft plug, today!)

Of course, with my long association with Paul
Allen, and his love of music, I've certainly learned a
thing or two in this area. I'm not just your typical
forty-something businessman...Impressive though
new Microsoft Music Producer is, it will never match
this hot new group from England that I've discovered. They're called Mike and the Mechanics, and
apparently Europe is going mad for their style of

music, which is called "Britpop." A guy called Mike and his older brother Noel formed the band last year and they have this really tempestuous, but deeply creative, high-bandwidth relationship (kinda like me and Paul). Their new single, called "The Living Years," may be somewhat influenced by Lennon and McCartney, but I just love it. I was surprised that no one in the office has heard of them yet. As always, I'm just too far ahead of my time...

"Man with no Windows will be forever in the dark." CONFUCIUS

MONDAY, JANUARY 13

Bad news for Leisure-Suit Larry (billionaire CEO of that OTHER software company), as he spent the day in court (Note: can't crush many competitors there, Larry!) over his alleged affair with onetime employee Adelyn Lee. (Allegedly he fired her days after their last date, for not sleeping with him.)

Dear Larry:
Wanna get married? If so, please send me one fourteen-carat diamond ring, one Acura NSX, one twenty-bedroom house, and some money to play the stock market.

Adelyn xoxoxo

Take a tip from me, Larry...if you're going to sleep with the staff, you better be more careful. Or marry them. Like I did. Hey, being married is way more efficient...I don't have to think about who I'm sleeping with tonight. Allegedly, he replied:

Adelyn...

NO!

Larry

P.S.: You're fired.

Melinda's so sad today: her beloved *Cosmo* magazine just dumped longtime editor Helen Gurley Brown. Hey, it's obvious! You can't be a seventy-five-year-old spinster and edit a magazine for raunchy twenty-four-year-olds. (Or rich, raunchy thirty-two-year-olds.) Duh...

TUESDAY, JANUARY 14

Back to Mungo Park...The space shuttle *Atlantis* docked with Russia's *Mir* space station to pick up U.S. astronaut John Blaha and drop off his replacement, Jerry Linenger. As they closed in on *Mir*, the *Atlantis* crew tried out a revolutionary space exercise machine—a free-floating treadmill that looks like a magic carpet. NASA wants to use the device aboard the international space station where delicate microgravity experiments can easily be upset by the vibration of exercise. The device uses gyro-

scopes to keep it steady during workouts. Sounds way cool. I WANT ONE! Just name your price, NASA, I think I can afford it!

I've started rereading *The Private Life of Chairman Mao*. Now that was a guy who was REALLY in charge. Maybe I go too easy on people at work.

Only two push-ups today. I hurt my arm rearranging the giant photo of the Pentium processor in my office.

WEDNESDAY, JANUARY 15

Melinda's STILL ticked off about that anniversary thing. She made me write "I must not forget our anniversary!" 500 times. Doesn't she know about cut and paste?

"But, honey, I've got a multibillion dollar software company to run" made her even angrier. Chicks, huh?

Slept in one of the spare bedrooms. Again.

THURSDAY, JANUARY 16

Why does the world want Microsoft to fail? All those negative New Year articles—"Does Bill have feet of clay?" and "Could this be the bad year for Microsoft?"—are out. And once again I'll answer them with a resounding "No!" and "Not this year, boys." They've even cited our dropping of the

Microsoft Home brand as some kind of big failure! Here's the truth on that one: I never, never, NEVER approved that artwork. (I blame Patty "Microsoft Bob Is Cool" Stonesifer for this one.) I didn't. Never. So I ditched the brand just as soon as I found out. All right?

Oh, apparently it's LIAM and his older brother Noel...So, why are they called MIKE and the Mechanics? That's just the stupidest thing I've ever heard.

FRIDAY, JANUARY 17

Bad news for Steve Case over at AOL (or America Offline, as I like to call it)...His new flat-rate pricing policy is causing MAJOR network traffic congestion, downtime, lack of access, and a whole bunch of other hassles. Ha! What good is having eight million users (another made-up-number alert?) if they can't use the system? Hey, Steve, do you know how to spell CLASS ACTION SUIT? Hey, AOLers! Get on over to my MSN now, and you'll have NO problems!

Good news for Bill Gates (ME!) over at Microsoft (or world's best-loved software corporation, as I like to call it)...Record revenues! Record earnings! Now that's COOL! Surely, NOW I'll get that raise...

Tonight I did five push-ups! Three, then one... then one more, two hours later, just before bed.

SATURDAY, JANUARY 18

I just heard that Iomega have laid off 1,000 employees in Utah because it's cheaper to manufacture in the Far East. That's what I call Bill-style management!

And check THIS out, control freaks! Madonna is banning her kid from watching TV and surfing the Internet. Baby Lola is already surfing the Internet? Amazing! Madonna obviously knows something about child care that Melinda and I don't, because Baby Jennifer (Melinda won't let me call her Baby Bill anymore) still shows absolutely no interest in becoming a part of the on-line revolution. Perhaps it's that conical, double-barreled baby feeding equipment she's been using!

Found that Victoria's Secret underwear in the dust-rags bag. If Melinda didn't want them, I could have tried them myself. Ha, ha.

SUNDAY, JANUARY 19

I've redesigned the push-up in a way that requires 57% less muscular power. Did ten!

Today, Melinda and I chatted on-line (using supercool Microsoft Chat). What better way to keep up with family news? Melinda also talked clothes... She wants to update my image. She thinks that I should be a Gap guy. Apparently, this store does all kinds of cool stuff like khakis and wild turtlenecks— in gray, navy blue, charcoal, forest green—that are really "me." She talked me into ordering a new button-down oxford, but I couldn't find the Gap home page. These guys are still in the dark ages! Picture the scene, in our digital future: I'm on Letterman being interviewed about *The Road Ahead II,* in my stylish Gap khakis...the viewers are impressed... they click on my pants to get the full info, and...no link. Way uncool!

I've almost decided to give up drinking Coke. My body is a temple.

"Man is still the most extraordinary computer of all."

JOHN F. KENNEDY

MONDAY, JANUARY 20

MARTIN LUTHER KING DAY

I haven't heard from Philippe Kahn for a while, but he's sent me a New Year's card. (Late, like most Kahn products!) Ah, how sweet. It's one of those Shoebox cards. You know... "a tiny little division of Hallmark." It says: "Congratulations on your latest $billion..." Thanks, Philippe. It looks like the barbarian at the gates of Microsoft is finally turning over a new leaf.

And inside..."I'd wish you good luck, but the prophet Nostradamus has already predicted your success...He said that around the year 2000 a terrible dictator would emerge and enslave the world in his evil grip, until he was finally overthrown and executed. I just assumed it was you." Ha, ha. Very funny, Philippe...Can you spell LOSER?

TUESDAY, JANUARY 21

Well, the latest Microsoft Office is finally out there, facing the world alone. I really hope that everyone enjoys using it just as much as I've enjoyed developing it. The press (usually due to its utter stupidity) constantly amazes me—and this launch has been no different. The recurring theme is "Microsoft Office has 83% of the office suite market...where can Microsoft go from here?" They obviously haven't been paying much attention during the past twenty years. When did I last allow 17% of a market to slip through my fingers?

WEDNESDAY, JANUARY 22

Of course, I was just joking about that last 17% market share...In the early days, I did think the natural market share for us was 100%, but as I get older and more mature I realize that free market competition is a good thing. In fact, I'm very happy with only 90% to 95% market share. And crushing the competition? Nah...Just SQUEEZING them is perfectly acceptable. That's why I'm going out of my way to keep Apple alive (I mean why else would I have a Mac Product Unit—after all these years—for just 5% of the market?), and doing a banking-related joint venture with Intuit. It's because I'm a nice guy, at heart...(Plus, it doesn't hurt to have the Justice Department watching! Boy, I'm so smart!)

Scorpio: your financial outlook for today is good. Coool! Even the stars love me...

THURSDAY, JANUARY 23

I've seen some pretty ridiculous look-and-feel cases in my time (occasionally instigated by me), and, I'll admit, sometimes it's been me defending stuff I probably didn't have a claim on...

But check this out...Microsoft Outlook (it's great, go out and get it now in new Microsoft Office!) has a little note feature that allows the user to create small notes with different colored backgrounds...Yup, you've guessed it! 3M, owner of Post-It Notes, is suing over "small-yellow-notey-type-thing-look-and-feel." Can you believe it? Could it be something to do with the huge flop that is their new electronic Post-It Note software? Maybe I caused them "irreparable harm" in a past life. Stay tuned for more developments...

Good news landed on my desk this morning in the form of an Internet/Intranet market report from Zona Research. They reckon that the market will grow from $20.5 billion this year to $42 billion by 1999. Cool! So, what could be better than a huge slice of a massive pie? How about an eat-the-whole-pie-in-one-go slice of a GIGANTIC pie! Hey, it's strategic thinking like this that's got me where I am today...

Aaaargh! Bad news landed on my desk this afternoon. No, this can't be happening...the traitor... How could he do this to me? It's *Forbes* magazine. With Ballmer on the front cover! No wonder he's been avoiding me. Doing front covers of major magazines is part of MY job description! And who writes this stuff? "Without this guy, Bill Gates would be a lot less rich." I don't think so...And "The General Patton of software." Huh? And "In the Putnam national mathematics competition for undergraduates, Ballmer outscored Gates." THIS IS JUST NOT TRUE! How can they make up these LIES about me? EVERYONE knows I'm the SMARTEST guy at Microsoft...

Why don't I take over Apple? Having conquered the software industry in almost all aspects, I could go into hardware. Wouldn't that be the final link in my success chain? Building my own PCs and putting all our own software on them. That sounds like total domination to me. With my knack for turning a profit, I could probably turn that company around in no time. I'll mull it over in background mode for a couple of months...

Hey, maybe I should buy the Packers? Paul has the Trailblazers. I should have my own team...

SUNDAY, JANUARY 26

Melinda went to Barnes & Noble. She bought me two books (I think they were reduced in a clearance sale). *Puerto Vallarta Squeeze* is another stirring love story from Robert James Waller. (I loved *Bridges of Madison County*.) *A Brief History of Time* by Stephen Hawking: how come I don't have this already? It's cool, although the math is a little simple for my taste. Apparently, there were no new books about me.

And there was some big sports thing...Oh, yeah, the Super Bowl. Give me Visual Basic any day...

Went a whole day without thinking about Steve Jobs...

"Money doesn't always bring happiness. People with $40 billion are no happier than people with $10 billion." BILL G.

Yeaaahhhh! I told you MSN2 was cool! We just got reviewed by *PC World* for their top ISPs feature and got an A+ and "Best Buy"! While IBM (losers!) only got a C– for their pathetic offering, the IBM Internet Connection! And AOL (I bet Steve's totally bummin' on this one) got a devastingly un-hip D—I guess it's true that AOL sucks. Ha! The transformation is complete...MSN's gone from a dead-before-it-started commercial on-line service to one of the largest ISPs. And it was easy...I just gave away the software with Windows and waited for the people to come. What a great strategy! What a great guy!

Oops... Major executive information-system failure...(And whoever's responsible can kiss their stock options good-bye.) Looks like it was MSN that got the C–(I guess I won't be getting a quarter from my pop, now, huh?) and IBM Internet Connection that got the A+. I know, it's hard to believe. But, hey, grades don't mean everything. We have a sexier home page and WAY more content. (And no matter what grade they get, IBM ain't EVER getting an icon on the Windows Desktop!) And we ALL know that (a) *PC World* is an anti-Microsoft propaganda tool and (b) it always takes us to Version 3 to get it completely right! (I guess I better look out for a new Usenet group...alt.msn.sucks!)

Melinda says that my fitness regime is already paying dividends. Apparently, last night, my stamina was awesome!

WEDNESDAY, JANUARY 29

I think I'll call CVS and negotiate the electronic rights for all films developed nationwide. Think of the possibilities...

The builders told me about further delays on the house. Jeez, why can't people stick to their deadlines? They assure me it'll be completely done before the end of the year, even if they have to cut out some features.

THURSDAY, JANUARY 30

I always enjoy bringing a completely new technology to market...empowering users, pushing the envelope, and, you've guessed it, crushing...oops, I mean squeezing...a competitor when they're down! Check this out...

There's an itty-bitty UK company called Psion that develops a teeny-weeny palmtop thing based on Z80 technology (come back CP/M, all is forgiven). Apparently, this is the official PDA of the Third World or something. Now, here's where it gets good.

We license Microsoft AutoRoute to them...or should I say we USED to license AutoRoute to them. Hee, hee, hee.

We've stopped. They asked why. We said, "Because all new PDA-based versions of AutoRoute will only be available for Windows CE." Being the nice guys we are, we added, "Are you developing a Windows CE machine?" They replied, "A what"?

Duh! Stay awake, Psion!

FRIDAY, JANUARY 31

More good news from Zona Reseach! (Who are these guys anyway? Do we own them, or something?) Their latest report is all about IE and how we've surged to 28% market share (up from only 1% four weeks ago: impressive growth even by Microsoft standards.) Netscape is DEFINITELY falling...Netscape is DEFINITELY getting squeezed ...Hey, Marc! Enjoy that Mercedes while you can still afford it!

I'm curious how an outside company like Zona can count the copies of IE, while inside Microsoft we've totally lost track. It wasn't like this in the old days when I did the accounting. Still, what a great time to renegotiate our Spyglass deal...I mean why should we pay royalties anyway—we don't get any money for IE, so why should they? And anyway, after all the development we've done it's more like our code anyway. Sheesh! I could write a browser over the weekend using Excel macros! (And $8 million? I look at it this way...Is it worth $8 million to "squeeze" Netscape?)

I wonder how Larry's doing in his lawsuit. I've been thinking, maybe he's home free. Surely no jury could ever believe that old cod eyes ever has (or even thinks about) sex!

A more long-running lawsuit has just gone to the jury: that O.J. civil case should finally be over. And then those journalists can get back to more important things—like writing about ME! Yeaaaahhhhh!

SATURDAY, FEBRUARY 1

Yo! I crush an on-line competitor...American Cybercast—creator (in the loosest sense of the word) of 'The Spot' and...errm, many other on-line dramas—has filed for Chapter 11 bankruptcy protection and canned the staff. Losers! Cue "Another One Bites the Dust" theme tune!

What a great night! Had a date with Melinda! I managed to persuade her that she wanted to "feel the force"...So, I took her to see the shiny new version of *Star Wars*. Twenty years later, the story of the battle between freedom-loving rebels and the evil empire is still awesome. Cooool! (Melinda seemed fascinated by Darth Vader's big helmet...so afterward, I breathed real heavy and let her play with my light saber.)

GROUNDHOG DAY

Melinda told me a joke today. I think she's trying to make a point, I just can't figure out what. That's chicks for you...even a brain-the-size-of-a-planet like me can't figure them out! So here it is...

A guy was crossing a road one day when a frog called out to him and said, "If you kiss me, I'll turn into a beautiful princess." So he bent over, picked up the frog, and put it in his pocket.

The frog spoke up again and said, "If you kiss me and turn me back into a beautiful princess, I will stay with you forever." The guy took the frog out of his pocket, smiled at it, and returned it to his pocket.

The frog then cried out, "If you kiss me and turn me back into a princess, I'll do ANYTHING you want." Again the guy took the frog out, smiled at it, and put it back into his pocket.

Finally, the frog demanded, "What's the matter? I've told you I'm a beautiful princess, that I'll stay with you forever, and that I'll do anything you want. Why won't you kiss me?"

The guy said, "Look, I'm Bill Gates, I really don't have time for a beautiful princess...but a talking frog is cool!"

"No one can earn a million dollars honestly."

WILLIAM JENNINGS BRYAN

MONDAY, FEBRUARY 3

It's often a lonely existence I lead as the world's richest, most powerful man. The pressures of fame force me and my family to seal ourselves inside a big, protective, bubble-like, capsulated shield thing (a.k.a. Bill's $50 million bunker).

But it's not always been like this. Up until a couple of years ago you could find me listed in the Seattle phone book. But the thousands of calls from enthusiastic fans I received every evening just forced me to switch to an unpublished number. And this made me real sad: in Seattle an unpublished number is much more expensive than in California. If, for example (suspend disbelief for a moment), Steve Jobs got loads of fan calls, he could switch to an unlisted number for around a THIRD of the price that it costs me!

It's even worse now. I hardly get any calls! When the phone does ring, it's usually a wrong number and the caller, amazingly, doesn't want to talk to me! There are other problems, too. If there's an emergency at Microsoft, how can they contact me at home? And what about long-lost friends trying to look me up?

So here's my solution and, as usual, it's a great big Bill-style rock 'n' roll problem-solver: I'm going to list my home phone number again, but I'm going to charge anyone who calls. (How about 1-900-ITS-BILL?) Pretty cool, huh? Here's my (very reasonable) scale of call charges...Between 9 A.M. and 5 P.M. you can reach me at home for just $5.00 per minute. After 5 P.M. (until bedtime) it's $10.00 per minute. And after bedtime I'm a good-value, premium-brand $25.00 per minute, with a generous 10% discount available to members of my immediate family, law enforcement agencies, members of royal families, and supermodels wanting to talk about the Internet. I'm also offering a 5% discount to nonprofit organizations (to make up for the loss of the Microsoft charity discount scheme). There's also a three minute minimum...but I may introduce a discount for voice mail messages.

Wow, this is such a great idea! Maybe I'll write about it in my *New York Times* syndicated column!

TUESDAY, FEBRUARY 4

So, O.J.'s guilty, huh? What a surprise! And $8.5 million in damages...Hey, if Melinda really could get half by divorcing me, I'd have to think carefully about all my "alternatives." Let's talk a nice round $30 million in fines...that's still only 1% of my fortune. (Or is it 0.1%? These decimal points always get me.)

But of course, she doesn't get half! My hotshot lawyers at Audacious, Brazen, and Crass (just my little joke, guys) have taken care of that problem with the longest, most complicated prenuptial agreement in history. (How complicated? Well, let's just say that Steve Ballmer is completely baffled by it. How long? Well, let's just say that it makes our software license agreements look short, reasonable, and fair.)

WEDNESDAY, FEBRUARY 5

Boy, I'm clocking up the miles this week! Yesterday it was Germany, launching our new Exchange Server to the sausage-eating krauts, today it's helping King Chirac of France drag the Gauls kicking and screaming into the electronic age. Who knows where I'll be tomorrow? I guess I've wired the civilized world and now it's Europe's turn.

I was surfing the Internet today, and boy, this thing is supercool! As a public service, I've carefully surfed, scanned, reviewed, and cataloged the Net. (Who needs a search engine?) So here are my Top Ten Internet Sites—check 'em out boys and girls...

1. **Microsoft.** What a surprise! This is a way-cool corporate site. Awesome, in fact.

2. **MSNBC.** The only news you'll need...

3. **MSN.** The coolest on-line service ever (perfect for disgruntled AOLers). Humor, insight, entertainment...Into orbit!

4. **Slate.** This Webzine rocks. Even without the naked chicks and Gillian Anderson interview.

5. **Corbis.** Wow! Such great graphics! World-famous art! Who came up with this cool idea? (I did. Yeaaahhhh!)

6. **Teledesic.** Awesome satellite site! Me and Craig are just such great guys, huh?

7. *The Road Ahead.* What a great book. What a great author. Boy, I'm so smart! (Don't forget! Buy it!)

8. **Amazon.com Books.** The world's biggest bookstore. And they stock *The Road Ahead* (just $11.16, you save $4.79 or 30%). Way cool!

9. **Gates/Walls.** It's the house that Bill built! Not just cool...fifty million dollars of cool!

10. **Microsoft.** So good I named it twice!

THURSDAY, FEBRUARY 6

One of the many cool things about Microsoft is our belief in diversity. We've even got a Diversity Department full of Diversity Managers to help implement a Diversity Mission. We're currently involved with all kinds of diverse projects such as setting up Web sites for Black American educational groups and diverse stuff like that. (And don't forget: we're hiring lots of chicks too!)

That's what makes the software industry so great. Diversity. Imagine what a dull world it would be if Microsoft was the only choice in software!

FRIDAY, FEBRUARY 7

Complain, moan, groan, pick fault, bitch, etc., etc. Yup, those press people are at it again... We release the most powerful suite of PC applications EVER and the industry grudgingly accepts this... then spends pages and pages complaining that Word 97 files can't be read by Word 95 unless users install a file converter (it's free, so what's the big deal?) available from our Web site. Does this really cause users big problems? Does it? I don't think so. In fact, I'm so convinced this isn't a problem, I'll PERSON-ALLY* visit anyone who's having trouble and convert the files for them!

And while I'm on the subject of those press guys, here's the latest quote they've attributed to me: "There are people who don't like capitalism, and there are people who don't like PCs, but there's no one who likes the PC who doesn't like Microsoft." Ha! What about the people that don't like PCs? They like Microsoft too. And what about those who don't like capitalism, but do like PCs? It's all just way too illogical... There's no way I could have said that!

(*Void where prohibited. Some restrictions apply. Offer only valid for sites with a 25,000 user—or higher—Site License for Microsoft Office 97. No academic, government, or nonprofit sites.)

Did I mention that AOL announced a $155 million loss for the quarter? C-ya, Steve!

Did I mention the great new Barney the Dinosaur–Microsoft licensing deal? Everyone loves Barney the Dinosaur!

What a great week!

Made a quick visit to EB (Electronics Boutique, stupid!) today and checked that Office was occupying its rightful 87% of the office suite shelf space. Luckily for EB, it was!

Next to the rows of Office were copies of that "ActiveOffice" Office add-on thing from SPC and get this: the product was selling for just $39.95—BUT they're offering a $50 mail-in rebate! Wake up guys! You're supposed to have the user pay YOU for the software, not the other way around!

But wait! Using my legendary lateral thinking (that Bill "vision thing") I see some real applications for this marketing strategy...Hey, I know Internet Explorer is already free, but why not have a $20 mail-in rebate? That way the user can either pay Netscape to use Navigator, or have us pay HIM (or her, sorry Melinda) to use Explorer. Cunning, huh? That's capitalism for you! That should get rid of that annoying Andreessen kid!

SUNDAY, FEBRUARY 9

Deep trouble with Melinda tonight. Ann (Winblad) called me at home, but used the "helping Bill with his book" excuse. Too bad it's been out for a while—even Melinda couldn't miss that one. (And if you don't yet have your copy of *The Road Ahead*... buy it, OK?)

"Only two things are infinite: the universe and human stupidity." ALBERT EINSTEIN

MONDAY, FEBRUARY 10

More bad (or is it good?) news from Apple... Seems that in a last, desperate bid for survival they're "restructuring"—corporate speak for laying off half the employees and selling noncompetitive divisions. That could cause big problems...does Apple have a competitive division that it can keep?

But I may have some good news for the 50% who are clearing their desks down in Cupertino... Microsoft is hiring! Come work for me—and a real company with real products, free soft drinks, stock options that are actually worth something, and loads of other cool stuff!

Latest news from the Madonna camp. Baby Mother Theresa Venezuela, or whatever she's called, is being sent to school in England...and she's going to be WALKING to school. She's a couple of months old, she can walk already, she's ready to enter the educational system...and she's prepared to live in a foreign country! I certainly believe in pushing kids toward success, but Madonna, hang on! Slow down! Jennifer's not even out of diapers yet. (Hey, Madonna! Got a Microsoft Barney the Dinosaur ActiMate yet? It's great!)

TUESDAY, FEBRUARY 11

Maybe an alliance is called for. Evita: the CD-ROM, the Web site...and think of all that back catalog. She's even got her hands on Alanis Morissette. Hmmm, she is old though. And she's lost all her dress sense: she hasn't been seen in black lace fingerless gloves since the mid-eighties.

More on Apple...I got a cool report today...Finally, we've cracked Apple's last hiding place—education! Last year, we moved ahead with 56% of the grade school computer market. And the Web browser of choice for our nation's educators? Here's a clue. It's not Netscape—and there aren't any others! I rule, yet again! The report ended with, "Apple officials could not be reached for comment." Why? There's nobody steering the ship!

More developments in Larry's court thing...Apparently, in a new e-mail that's been discovered, he described Adelyn as the "Spandex Queen" and referred to himself as "president of the Amateur Gynecology Club." Now that kind of thing is absolutely outrageous. But that's Oracle for you. Luckily, stuff like that could never happen at Microsoft...

WEDNESDAY, FEBRUARY 12

ASH WEDNESDAY, LINCOLN'S BIRTHDAY

So much for the Web being the new rock 'n' roll...As far as I can tell, it's still the rock dudes who get the hot chicks. Latest news from England is that Liam from Mike and the Mechanics is tying the knot with Patsy Kensit—young, hot English chick of *Lethal Weapon 2* fame. (Or is it 2 *Lethal Weapons* fame, ha, ha!)

You know, since getting into Mike and the Mechanics I've become a regular Dr. Pop. Look out for new albums from wrinkly old rockers Depeche Mode and U2. They've had more albums than MS Word has version numbers! At least I'm growing old gracefully...Who wants to see a balding old dude strut around on stage wearing leather pants and mirrored shades (apart from Jerry Hall)? Not me! So, old rockers, go back to Europe and let new blood like Mike and his Mechanics have a fair shot at the U.S. market...

THURSDAY, FEBRUARY 13

Microsoft Investor is OFFICIALLY the fastest growing, free, personal investment site on the Web—with over 700,000 hits per day. Now, that's what I call cool.

But there are still a couple of places where I'm not the top dog...For example, according to *Slate,* I'm a miserable twelfth in the list of Highest (Annual) Charitable Donations with gifts of "only" $27 million, including $15 million to Harvard. I guess the charitable donations list is one of the few areas where it's prudent to be in the top twenty, but not the top ten.

Check this out, Bill trivia fans! The roof of my new place is built from the same kind of Cambrian slate that King Henry of England built his castle out of. Cool!

FRIDAY, FEBRUARY 14

ST. VALENTINE'S DAY

It's Valentine's Day. And I didn't forget. Melinda is just SO great! (But she's still not getting half.) I took her to Nathan's restaurant hobby, Rover's, where (as usual) Thierry Rautureau, the owner, fawned all over us, poured us champagne, fed us a dozen courses, and handed us a bill for $400! Chicks are just so expensive!

Which reminds me...So I have a long golfing weekend with Ann Winblad every year. So what? It's the nineties! Surely a man and a woman can have a platonic friendship without all that "are they, aren't they" stuff. She never even held my club!

Besides, Melinda has nothing to worry about. She knows that once I've upgraded, I NEVER reinstall the old version.

SATURDAY, FEBRUARY 15

I came across this big cult thing on the Web today. It's all about me. Cool! Apparently, there's this theory that I'm the center of Hollywood, the focal point around which all the stars gyrate! Way cool! Here's the scoop: I can be linked to any Hollywood film actor in less than five links.

Using this info you can work out the "Bill Factor" of any celebrity. And the weird thing? All these links happen through some actor named Kevin Bacon! Try it out. Think of an actor...say, Gene Hackman...Gene Hackman was in *The Firm* with Tom Cruise...Tom Cruise was in *A Few Good Men* with Kevin Bacon...and I met this Kevin Bacon guy at a party last year! Supercool!

I'm told that working out the Bill Factor for all these actors is a cool game that's spreading across the world like wildfire. More fame for me! And it might help Microsoft take over Hollywood, too!

SUNDAY, FEBRUARY 16

Of course, lots of the stuff that I see while surfing the Web just isn't worth the server space... Pitiful content, no design skills, and generally embarrassing—especially for someone with my keen aesthetic sense. So here's my Top Ten Worst Sites of the Web—AVOID AT ALL COSTS!

1. **Netscape.** A vanity home page for some kid called Marc Andreessen—and his homemade Web browser. Get a life, Marc!

2. **The Secret Diary of Bill Gates.** This pathetic material doesn't deserve band-width or server space. It doesn't sound anything like me...

3. **Boycott Microsoft Page.** An exercise in futility. Ha!

4. **Apple.** Get Steve "the Visionary" Jobs to fix this site!

5. **Intuit.** A home finance page put together by a former fat salesman? 'Nuff said.

6. **AOL.** It's true—AOL sucks!

7. **Justice Department.** Can't stop me, can't build a decent Web site either.

8. **IBM.** Oh dear, oh dear.

9. **Oracle.** Give it up, Larry.

10. **Encyclopaedia Britannica.** Too little, too late. Too bad.

"Forgive your enemies, but never forget their names."

JOHN F. KENNEDY

MONDAY, FEBRUARY 17

PRESIDENTS' DAY

Presidents' Day? Ha! Keep 'em working, that's what I say...

Did the keynote at the (unbelievably boring) annual AAAS meeting in Seattle in the morning. The amazing thing about computer science is that the hardware and software combination that's created is a tool, the best tool that's ever been created for leveraging human innovation. There's probably no business like it in the sense that with Moore's Law–type improvements in chip technology, our opportunity to do more in software goes up very, very rapidly. And then we can charge more! Yeaaahhhhh!

Then I went to Barnes & Noble to buy a copy of *Time* (nothing about me this week) and look for more books about...well, about me, actually. Nothing new, but plenty of copies of the Randall Stross masterpiece *The Microsoft Way*. He loves me!

TUESDAY, FEBRUARY 18

Since we announced our new Barney ActiMate, there have been two big questions that people keep asking...

The first: Why is Microsoft getting into toys? Well, you know, it's NOT a TOY! It's an EARLY LEARNING SYSTEM in the shape of a plush purple dinosaur. Through Barney, children will learn the alphabet, the meaning of shapes and colors, how to play games such as peek-a-boo, and other developmental skills. I've tested it extensively in the Jennifer Usability Lab and it was just GREAT—until she tried to eat it...and then threw up.

And second: Who do you think would win in a fight, Barney the Dinosaur ActiMate or Tickle Me Elmo? You know, sometimes I think people don't take me entirely seriously...

WEDNESDAY, FEBRUARY 19

Oh boy, oh boy, oh boy! I've seen the light! Forget Mike and his boring Mechanics...Forget Cindy Crawford (especially now she's thirty and tubby), Jennifer Aniston and all those other third-rate girlies ...My views on music and chicks have changed forever...Because today, I saw...THE SPICE GIRLS!!!!

OK, you probably know that when I get bitten by a bug, I get bitten big! For example, last year just flew by as I devoted almost all my energy to Microsoft's new Internet strategy. Well, this year I'm really pushing the envelope...it's time for Microsoft to get a SPICE GIRLS strategy. They're gonna be big. Huge. Bigger than Office. Bigger than the Internet. Maybe even as big as me! Here's my ten-point action plan:

1. Get our U.K. office to prepare a detailed report on what a "Zig-a-Zig...Ahhh" is.

2. And prepare a report on what "Posh" as in "Posh Spice" means in English. (Does it mean horny?)

3. Find out all their e-mail addresses.

4. Ditch that USELESS dinosaur thing and launch a range of "Baby Spice" electronic toys...I mean EARLY LEARNING SYS-TEMS for kids.

5. Use my influence at the White House and in European government circles to get "Sporty Spice" replaced...then I'll have the hots for all five!

6. Buy the record on CD, cassette, minidisc, CD-ROM, DCC, DVD...

7. Add a SPICE GIRLS listening room to my house plans.

8. Call Kevin Bacon for info on hot Hollywood parties that the SPICE GIRLS may be at. I'm a party animal! Grrrrr...

9. Get Corbis on the case for electronic rights to all the pics. (Especially the ones of Geri Spice from the *London Sun*.)

10. Read up on Margaret Thatcher. Maybe she's a babe, too!

FRIDAY, FEBRUARY 21

Introduced sit-ups to my fitness regime. Abs of steel, here I come...I must buy something like the Abdominizer, or the Ab Isolator...ordinary sit-ups are just too low tech.

Spent a few hours surfing the Net. I can't believe how much stuff there is about me. But it's so negative. Why do they hate me so? There are Microsoft hate pages and cruel jokes about Windows. I was so upset I had to go and look at my bank statement...

My SPICE GIRLS world domination predictions are coming true! Not only are they #1 in the charts, they're the only five-girl band from London to ever have the WHOLE of suck.com devoted to them. And they're in *Time* too! (Although they didn't make the cover like you-know-who...) Spice-tastic!

WASHINGTON'S BIRTHDAY

It's official! I'm richer than Ecuador, Sri Lanka, Bulgaria, and Iraq! Eat my dust, Saddam! And, check out my growth rate...I'm up $10 billion in the past twelve months alone! I could buy the entire output of new Ferraris for the next thirty-four years and still have change for insurance and servicing! Hmmm... that's a little decadent. Maybe I'll just stick with the twenty I currently own.

My position at the top of the *Forbes* chart just gets safer and safer...New number three, Paul Sacher, the Swiss cuckoo clock magnate, is ninety years old...so he's not gonna be around much longer. And, let's face it, WarrenB ain't no spring chicken! There's NO WAY that Melinda can leave me for a RICHER guy! (Or a better looking one. But my natural modesty stops me from saying that.)

If you wannabe my lover, got to get with my friends. Make it last forever, friendship never ends...Damn! Will I never get that tune out of my head?

"I really really wanna wanna zig-a-zig, ahhhhh..."

SPICE GIRLS

MONDAY, FEBRUARY 24

Good news from the Internet camp...I found this HOT, NEW Web site. It's called "BillBoard" and it's all about ME! Wow! That's just so cool! It's part of the awesome Microsoft site, and I'm the ONLY Microsoft employee to get his very own, PERSONAL page. (Even Ballmer doesn't get one. Oh no.) Billtastic!

Bad news from the Spice camp...It was revealed today that VictoriaB (a.k.a. "Posh Spice") didn't sing a note on their supercool #1 hit, "Wannabe." I know just how she must feel...For years people have been alleging that I didn't write a line of code in our supercool #1 hit, MS-DOS.

TUESDAY, FEBRUARY 25

Hey, at least I'm still a hit with the cyber babes... This just came in over the transom:

> Dear Bill:
> If you ever need a cyber tryst, this computer weenie-ette is a total fox!! And I don't require the usual necessities of the traditional "kept"

47

woman like the apartment, the Jaguar, the credit cards, the complimentary software. Just ride me, big stallion!! YEEE-HAAAAAAAA!

So, I replied...

Hey, Grrrl:
Yeaaahhhh! A young, hot babe, writing to me! And I'm glad that you're not a material girl. Cheap is good. (Very good.) I don't know what a "cyber tryst" is, but I'm sure it's going to be fun. Yeaaahhh!

But I'm surprised you know about the "big stallion" thing—it's Melinda's pet name for me. But I guess she told some of her friends...And they told some of their friends...And then they told some of their friends...And pretty soon, the whole software industry knows.

YEEE-HAAAAAAAA! Bill G.

Wow! This biotech stuff really is supercool...A little Scottish company has succeeded in creating the first clone of an adult animal! (Too bad I didn't have stock in the Roslin Institute instead of Darwin Molecular...Wake up, Darwin! What have you guys been doing?) Dolly the sheep is the identical twin of her genetic mother, grown from a single cell of her udder. And think of the wonderful applications of this discovery...What about more Bills? That's right! Think how great Microsoft would be if there were even more of me!

What is it with *Fortune*? They've made a list of the top movers and shakers, and...I'm NOT listed! That's totally random! Don't they know that I was PERSONALLY SUMMONED to Davos, Switzerland, for the annual meeting of the World Economic Forum to enlighten world political, business, and academic leaders about information technology? (That's how cool I am!)

Happy Birthday, Chelsea Clinton! I wonder if SHE wants to talk about the Internet?

FRIDAY, FEBRUARY 28

I don't understand how Steve Jobs keeps his cute and cuddly image intact when his negotiating strategies are so similar to mine...The facts? When Apple is almost down and out, and desperate for salvation, he sticks them with his NeXT OS, and gets $400 million. Then he negotiates a fat salary as an "adviser"—and only turns up for four hours a week! And THEN he forces Disney to tear up a deal that gives them a HUGE Office-style 90% of the profits from Pixar movies and settle for a mere 50%! How does he do it? Maybe I've been underestimating him?

Big day on the fitness front. Ten old-fashioned push-ups, ten low-tech sit-ups, and fifteen minutes on the trampoline. Phew!

SATURDAY, MARCH 1

The computer industry just isn't what it used to be. Take company names for instance. Read the name "Microsoft" and you know exactly what we do. We make software (the "soft" part) for micro-computers (the "micro" part).

Imagine the consumer confusion if we'd named ourselves after, say, a fruit. Banana? Pineapple? Nobody would ever buy a damn thing!

So why do these start-ups go for such ridiculous names? Take Kim Polecat (her name's pretty silly, too, but I guess she can't help that) down at Marimba... What a name! Did I call MSN "Glockenspiel"? Did I call it "Xylophone"? No! I went for a sensible name with meaning for the intended audience. Get real, Kim. People will be using ActiveX long after Java is remembered only as some place in the Third World somewhere. Think of a sensible name for your company!

Oh, yeah...And one more thing, Kim...You're a chick! Chicks can't do software companies! (Sorry, Melinda, but it's TRUE!) And if you don't believe me, take a look at Quarterdeck...

OK, so Baby Jennifer isn't grabbing all the celebrity baby headlines with all the stiff competition she's getting from the new additions to the Anderson-Lee, Jackson, and Madonna families. In fact, my revelation that I'm only going to leave her $10 million in my will only just managed to scrape the front pages. (I don't want Jennifer to grow up a spoiled child. She'll just have to learn to manage on the paltry $500,000 a year she'll get in interest. Yes, I know it's harsh, but she has to learn to be like ordinary people.)

But at least Jennifer doesn't come from a dysfunctional family. And—Baby Jackson, take note—at least her parents have actually done it!

"His is a historic level of genius." MICROSOFT PERSON ABOUT BILL GATES (GIVE THAT MAN A BONUS!)

The next leg of my Bill Gates, rock 'n' roll world tour continues...If it's Monday, it must be... INDIA! Third World superpower and intellectual factory of cheap MS programmers! I tried to buy the Taj

Mahal for Melinda (what a supercool gift!) but even for the "Sultan of Software," there's a limit. Bummer! Decided to list the most powerful guys on the planet. After me, that is.

1. **Bill Gates.** (OK, I couldn't resist.)

2. Hey, this Intellisense stuff really does work for numbered lists! **Paul Allen.**

3. Tie between **Steve Ballmer** and **Nathan Myhrvold.**

4. **Warren Buffett.**

5. **Rupert Murdoch.** (Content, content, content...)

6. **Jeffrey Katzenberg.**

7. **George Lucas.** (Thirty-three Academy Awards can't be wrong.)

8 **Steven Spielberg.** (Nice wife, too.)

9. **Bill #2.** (Hey, a mere politician makes the list!)

10. **Andrew Grove.** (Thanks for the picture, Andy!)

TUESDAY, MARCH 4

Discussed India's need for an information infra-structure, especially in telecommunications, over a leisurely breakfast with India's prime minister. So this is what it feels like to be a world leader...Pretty cool, huh?

Now it's more fun...My list of the down and outs...

1. **Schmidt at Novell.** (Jeez, who wants THAT job?)

2. **Jim Clark.** (Just kidding!)

3. **Steve Case.** (Eat my shorts, scumbag.)

4. **Steve Jobs.** (Personality-wise.)

5. That annoying **Andreessen** kid.

6. **Steve Jobs.** (NeXT is no more.)

7. **Scott Cook.** (Nothing personal. Intuit WILL die.)

8. **Doug Carlston.** (I never wanted Dr. Seuss anyway—it's for kids.)

9. **Steve Jobs.** (Even his parents didn't want him.)

10. **Everyone at Apple.** (Another Jobs baby dies?)

WEDNESDAY, MARCH 5

Gave the keynote address at the Industry Leadership Summit in Bombay. I'm so cool! So, how will technology changes impact India's 160,000 software developers over the coming years? Indian software developers are among the best in the world, but for India to really develop a presence in the world IT market, the local IT industry needs better infrastructure, access to the latest technology, and protection of intellectual property. (That means: Stop stealing Windows, you losers!)

Back home, it looks like Bill #2 got wind of my little plan—he's banned cloning research! That's so sad...Now I won't get to see Bill #3, #4, #5, and #6. (And I was feeling pretty confident, too. A few months working together, and we would have had ALL THE MONEY IN THE ENTIRE WORLD!!!)

And another thing...How come Bill #2 hasn't invited ME for a sleepover in the Lincoln Bedroom?

THURSDAY, MARCH 6

Phew! Now South Africa, for a two-day visit... A dynamic country spearheading the rest of Africa's growth into a "tiger" economy similar to the Far East. (That means: Buy more Windows!)

FRIDAY, MARCH 7

Things are going really well with Melinda. I decided to work on the clincher, and show her my sensitive side (everyone has one, even me). I wrote a poem about our wedding in Hawaii. Apparently, chicks love that mushy stuff...

the beach

toes curled in the wet sand
smelling the scent of the sea
i reach downward
and i think a perfect hand
might hold this perfect pebble
and, throwing, might trace
the perfect parabola
suspended, neatly in time
between the sunset
and the waves
then slowly dropping
like that perfect, fiery sun
reflected in these perfect waters
then lost to me
sinking to the sand
finally resting, perfectly
on this perfect beach.

Now will Melinda's software interface with my hardware? I think so...

SATURDAY, MARCH 8

Melinda is still in shock. The unexpected outpouring of poetic expression has left her stunned. However, it did seem to have the right effect, as she wouldn't let me go to the office this morning. This poetry stuff is way underrated. On the other hand, I can't stay in bed all day. Another week, another company to crush...

Hey! Maybe what you want (what you really really want) is to download...Sun's HotJava browser—the all-Java competitor for IE. I'm shaking in my boots! NOT!

No push-ups today. Way too tired.

SUNDAY, MARCH 9

Quiet day at home. Groceries at Shop 'n' Save (used all my coupons!). Rented a couple of videos and bought some ice cream. Went to Ben & Jerry's home page, ordered ten pints of Funky Monkey. Used Melinda's credit card in case the encryption isn't too secure. Watched *The Bridges of Madison County*. It's even better than the book. I wonder if Meryl Streep wants to talk about the Internet? Clint Eastwood is a little out of character, though. He plays the hero as the most sensitive, wonderful, loving, and glistening kind of man. Kinda like me with Melinda, I guess...And then *Infinity*, the awesome biopic of brash, eccentric wiz (and Nobel Prize winning physicist) Richard Feynman. Supercool.

"I have nothing to declare but my genius."

OSCAR WILDE (AND BILL G.)

ORTHODOX LENT BEGINS

So that's what happens when I leave the country…Everyone decides it's a great time to attack me and my company. "Bugs" in Windows. "Bugs" in ActiveX. And great big "bugs" in Internet Explorer. It's just not fair. And is it credible? So you're surfing along using supercool IE…Do you REALLY believe that it's possible for a malicious Web page to BLOW UP your PC? I don't think so.

I even found this e-mail…But too late! Oops!

Dear Bill:

We're two supersmart MIT computer jocks and we've found a NASTY, NASTY bug in IE that allows a rogue Web page to ZAP your PC. It's SCARY.

Get back to us ASAP, or we're going PUBLIC with our Web page BUG demo right away to alert the greatest number of people possible to the problem. You'll be sorry if you don't reply!

Sincerely, Tim & Chris at MIT

P.S.: We're having a real tough time getting enough beer in college. Some cash would help, OK?

TUESDAY, MARCH 11

We've just launched the preview of our hot, NEW version of Internet Gaming Zone! It's the great place to meet other like-minded gamers from around the world and challenge them to mind-blowing versions of all the latest hot games. And, boy, are these games HOT! We've got bridge, spades, chess, go, checkers, and more! WOW! Check it out! I bet John Romero's GREEN with envy!

We're even going to add Microsoft Monster Truck Madness...Into orbit! And, at the end of March, we're making backgammon available... Wicked!

I can't wait for a game of death-match multi-player bridge! Yeaaahhhhh! (And guess what? I'll have all the cheat codes! There's NO WAY I can lose playing this sucker! I'll sneak up behind WarrenB with the BFG. Just when he's holding all the aces! Supercool!)

WEDNESDAY, MARCH 12

Spring Internet World was a ZOO! My Internet thing has certainly arrived! It's hot!

It's taken some time, but my mission to wire the world seems to be working...Even the Queen of England got her own Web site last week! Perhaps there's hope for Europe and the rest of the Third

World after all! And what browser is Liz—Her Royal Highness—using? Well, it's not HotJava...And it's not Navigator...You've guessed it! Internet Explorer—as used by her total queen-ness the Queen of England! And, like me, she's got a real on-line sense of humor: her pages are coded in HRHtml! Supercool! Hmmm...Maybe I can get one of those cool "By Royal Appointment" logos? Queen-tastic!

THURSDAY, MARCH 13

I had no idea when I mentioned this cloning thing that the world's press would pick up on it...Wow! The whole cloning issue is really getting pretty heated! But hold on! Let's step back a moment ...So, over in England they've managed to clone a sheep. That's pretty cool. But how do they know they've REALLY cloned it? Aren't ALL sheep just kind of white, woolly, and dumb? (I must make some time to finish Watson's *Molecular Biology of the Gene*. I only got to page 99...Just 1,001 to go. The truth is in there...)

So you're surfing along using supercool IE... When a malicious Web page automatically starts up Windows Calculator! Ooh! Now THAT'S scary!

FRIDAY, MARCH 14

Wanna know how rich I am? Here's how rich I am...I'm walking along when a $100 bill drops out of my pocket and onto the ground. Should I bend over and pick it up? No way, Jose! Based on what my time is worth, if it takes me longer than 1.24 seconds to pick it up, I'm losing money! (On the other hand, a $100 bill, while small, is still REAL money. While, as you know, my Microsoft stock is only illusory "paper wealth" dependent upon the vagaries of the stock market. So, maybe I should pick it up. Just in case I need it later.)

SATURDAY, MARCH 15

WarrenB and I went to McDonald's for lunch
today. (Doing our unassuming billionaires shtick.) We pooled our vouchers and got two free Value Meals! (Phew! I didn't need that $100 bill after all!) Warren was concerned that we were going to lose coupon value due to the current burger wars...But I was convinced that Mickey D's would be offering full price-protection to customers such as ourselves who hold pre–burger war vouchers. Isn't capitalism great? God bless America! (And McDonald's, too!)

OK, OK, OK...Enough already! If you're that worried about security with IE—send it back and I'll refund EVERY CENT you paid for it...(Hey, I knew this free stuff would save me money in the long run!)

Went to the Gap with Melinda and bought more stuff with my Turbo-Platinum Ultra-Gold Bill Card. I'm just so smooth. No wonder the babes dig me. Here are my Top Ten Gap Clothing Items...

1. Sky blue turtleneck with long sleeves

2. Navy wool V neck with golfer motif

3. Cream button-down oxford shirt

4. Light chambray button-down oxford shirt

5. Gray button-down oxford shirt

6. Forest green polo shirt with short sleeves

7. Lemon button-down oxford shirt

8. Classic-cut Gap khakis—olive

9. Gray turtleneck with long sleeves

10. Classic-cut Gap khakis—stone

"Reality is merely an illusion, albeit a very persistent one."

ALBERT EINSTEIN

MONDAY, MARCH 17

ST. PATRICK'S DAY

Tragedy! Ginger Spice has suffered a horrific injury during a video shoot. Apparently she was digging around for a particularly juicy nugget of ear wax (off camera, of course) when she lost a false fingernail deep in her ear canal! It took three hours in intensive care to remove the offending article. I just hope her singing doesn't suffer...

And I've finally gotten a price for hiring the foxy fivesome...Mercedes-Benz coughed up $350,000 plus an SLK roadster each for just ten minutes last week. (Even by my standards, that's pretty good!) I wonder how long I'd get if I spend the rest of our corporate entertainment budget on a private Spice show? Or maybe I'll be cheap and just hire Sporty Spice to do a solo!

TUESDAY, MARCH 18

Today we announced Microsoft Active Accessibility. It's an operating system–based technology that makes it easier for software developers to write applications that can be used by people with disabilities, thus helping them use personal computers . . . and buy Microsoft software. We already have close to 90% market share in the able-bodied market segment, this way we can go all out for total domination of the spastic market. The disabled (blind, deaf, crippled) is a market ripe for exploitation, although I haven't yet figured out what we do for the intellectually challenged—they're too dumb to realize they need Microsoft software.

Boy, are we a caring, sharing software company or what! "A PC on Every Desk and Every Wheelchair..." I bet we get a humanitarian award for this initiative...

WEDNESDAY, MARCH 19

While I don't like to dwell on the past, sometimes there are useful lessons to be learned. History is full of examples of established companies and products that fell from grace because they didn't anticipate or adapt to new trends. I'll admit we're pretty dominant right now, but I have to keep looking over my shoulder for my next big rival. For example, I don't know how the world survived before we invented the Internet back in '96—luckily, all those other companies were just too slow to catch on to big trends.

THURSDAY, MARCH 20

A better example? David Cassidy of the Partridge Family...He was so cool. He was AWESOME. My sisters LOVED this guy. (It's a little-known fact that my sexy hairstyle and snappy dressing were inspired by David. Too bad he wasn't as good looking—or smart—as me.)

He was a big Microsoft-style #1 in the teen idol market, with a big Office-style 83% of the prepubescent yearning segment—yet failed to adapt to new developments in popular music. Why didn't he recognize the strategic inflection point in his career? Why didn't he realize that he was about to be undone by a 10X change in the entertainment world? Because he wasn't paranoid. And because he didn't ruthlessly crush his competitors—the Monkees, Andy Gibb, that Vanilla Ice Cream dude, Milli Vanilli, New Kids on the Street, and, of course, the Spice Girls, before they got established. The result? A one-way ticket on the Last Train to Nowheresville. But that won't happen to me...Oh, no. (And I had a crush on that Susan Dey, too. I wonder if SHE wants to talk about the Internet?)

If he'd put his songs on CD-ROM instead of those low-tech 45s he'd probably still be here today, making groovy tunes instead of guest spots on VH1 (the Apple of the music video channels).

FRIDAY, MARCH 21

Wow! Intel has developed the world's fastest supercomputer, able to perform one trillion operations every second! (That's 1.06 teraflops, jargon fans!) Basically it's a whole bunch of Pentium Pros in a box connected in parallel. (Well, 7,264 Pentium Pros to be precise.) Looks like Andy's trying to demonstrate that with standard building blocks you can deliver world-record-breaking power. Cool! I want one! Just watch Windows 98 fly on this baby!

And a joint venture with HP! Am I cool, or what? (Note: trick question—I am way cool.)

SATURDAY, MARCH 22

Melinda wants me to do a tour to promote Windows CE as the OS of choice for intelligent household appliances. And I'm always on the lookout for new form factors...Has Microsoft trademarked the SIVC (Simply Interactive Vacuum Cleaner) yet? She has dozens of ideas for how American life in the next century can be enriched by interactive Internet-enabled appliances based on MS software. For example, the SIVC, when operated by the future houswife, will automatically sense that it requires its virtual bag to be changed, and will e-mail the selected HAP (Household Appliance Provider), asking them to pay her a visit. Thanks, honey. What would I do without you?

SUNDAY, MARCH 23

PALM SUNDAY

Yeaaahhhh! We nailed the guy that was using the Internet to offer a version of our Office trial version—with the ninety-day time limit DISABLED. You know, if these Internet guys were honest (and those Arabs, Indians, and assorted Third World losers were on the level) I'd probably be worth $50 billion by now, instead of a paltry thirty. Software piracy is a terrible, terrible thing...

And, based on my recent press clippings, here's my Top Ten List of Things for Journalists to Go On and On and On About...

1. Bugs in Internet Explorer

2. Microsoft's TOO dominant

3. Is all that money really healthy for just ONE man?

4. Security problems with ActiveX

5. Windows CE: isn't it...well, crap?

6. What about file compatibility for Office95/97?

7. NTW & NTS...They're the same, right?

8. My teeny-weeny joke about the handicapped

9. Windows is late (again)

10. The Spice Girls are talentless no-hopers, OK?

"We know that the nature of genius is to provide idiots with ideas twenty years later."

HEAD OF XEROX PARC

MONDAY, MARCH 24

What do I want to write today? Founded in 1975, Microsoft (NASDAQ "MSFT") is the world-wide leader in software for personal computers. The company offers a wide range of products and services for businesses and personal use, each designed with the mission of making it easier and more enjoyable for people to take advantage of the full power of personal computing every day. What happened to "a Bill Gates book on every desk"? I think the PR guys have been tampering with my vision statement...

Am I officially the World's Richest Man yet? I bet Melinda's really proud of me now...I bet NOW she's happy that she dumped that Wrigley's Gum dude.

TUESDAY, MARCH 25

I've been watching the "competition" over at Netscape, and I can't help but notice that they've hardly been the guardians of stockholder value (unlike some people I could mention!) over the last year—a whopping 65% drop in stock price! Last year, Marc's parents must have been really proud when he told them he was worth $1.2 billion. ("Pretty good for a kid.") This year, all he can say is that he's lost $800 million ("How Marc?") and that he's down to his last $400 mil. ("Don't worry, WE still love you.") You gotta feel sorry for the kid... NOT! NOT! NOT! LOSER!!!!!!

WEDNESDAY, MARCH 26

Last night I woke up screaming, drenched in sweat. I had a major nightmare where Jobs, Kahn, and Reno fed me poisoned Kool-Aid and danced around me chanting: "OS 8, OS 8..." It was way harsh. Melinda made me a mug of warm milk, gave me a big hug, and calmed me down. I miss my mom...

In another example of Bill-style economics (NOT!), Quaker unloaded Snapple for just $300 million...They paid $1.7 billion for the company, less than three years ago, in what must be one of the worst deals in American corporate history. I'm surrounded by losers. No wonder I look so good!

THURSDAY, MARCH 27

Wow! More weirdness in the computer biz...Apparently driven insane by using Netscape Navigator as their preferred Web browser, thirty-nine members of a computer programming and Web page design cult committed mass suicide in San Diego. (So it's true: computer programming and Web page design can MESS YOU UP! Don't start, kids. Just say "NO.")

Hey! There's no way they can pin THIS on an IE security hole! My theory is that it was the subliminal messages in Navigator...These guys "shed their containers" to make a rendezvous with a UFO flying in the tail of the Hale-Bopp comet. Why didn't you take Marc and Larry with you?

So...I guess the good news is that there's a vacancy for a new Webmaster for their Heaven's Gate Web site...

FRIDAY, MARCH 28

GOOD FRIDAY

The Novell Developer's (so, there's still one left?) Conference finished today. Apparently, "Novell is focused and back as a contender." Right.

These guys are nowhere! And the new CEO, Eric Schmidt, has a big Apple-style turnaround job on his hands. Give it up now, Eric! My data shows that sales of our Windows NT Server grew by over 86% and outsold Novell NetWare by more than two times last year. My additional data shows overwhelming customer satisfaction with NT Server. And, finally, my other additional data shows that everyone agrees with me that Novell are a bunch of losers. (All data from IDC—so it must be true!)

SATURDAY, MARCH 29

I think Andy, over at Intel, has stolen my brilliant "help the disabled" plan. Apparently, he's already spent a lot of time with Stephen Hawking and given the guy a whole new hardware setup with "Intel Inside" plastered all over it. Great publicity… but I thought you were my friend, Andy.

Quick lunch down at the Taco Bell down on 4th—coupon for three soft tacos and a medium drink. A penny saved is a penny earned! Cooooool!

SUNDAY, MARCH 30

EASTER SUNDAY

Larry, Larry, Larry… Are you NUTS? (Or is this just another stunt in the man's eternal quest for self-publicity?) Surely he cannot be serious about acquiring Apple! The guy obviously has more money than he knows what to do with…On the other hand, if he's got his hands full with Apple he'll have less time to bother me. (And less time to go on about his stupid NC thing. And, incidentally, less time for fooling around with the staff—no bad thing.) Yeeahhh! GO FOR IT, LARRY!

Great Easter joke for Jennifer... What do you get if you pour boiling water down a rabbit hole? Hot cross bunnies...

"Grove giveth and Gates taketh away."

BOB METCALFE (INVENTOR OF ETHERNET)

MONDAY, MARCH 31

EASTER MONDAY (CANADA)

And another joint venture with Walt Disney... MSN's Disney's Daily Blast, the first major offering of kids' programming on the Internet by Disney Online. Children are an extremely important audience for us, representing an entirely new generation that will grow up wanting Microsoft software. Rock 'n' roll!

Watched *Toy Story* on video with Jennifer. Hey, it's not bad! Didn't it win an Oscar? I bet Steve Jobs is really proud...

TUESDAY, APRIL 1

Some of the guys at work filled my office with copies of Lotus SmartSuite as an April Fool's prank. Very funny, guys—of course I have a sense of humor! Can you spell NO MORE STOCK OPTIONS?

And a Swiss Web site, PC Tip, run by the International Data Group, caused a sensation today by posting the "special preview" version of IE5 (right!) on their April Fool's Web site... The downloads by gullible Microsoft worshippers were substantial—I even got a copy myself. Lawyers at dawn, I think...

WEDNESDAY, APRIL 2

Today, I gave the keynote at yet another tedious conference. It just reminds me how many people out there really love me. I mean, I'm a very lovable guy. (And rich too.) And I get to mention Moore's Law in a speech yet again... You know Moore's Law: the number of people talking about the improvement in processor performance will double every eighteen months.

I spent the night with Microsoft 3D Movie Maker, but I still couldn't get anything as good as *Toy Story* out of it. I guess Stevie paid his millions though, while I didn't pay a DIME for Movie Maker—as president I get special privileges like free evaluation software and free soda...

THURSDAY, APRIL 3

Bummer! Turns out EVERYONE at Microsoft gets free soda. No wonder profits aren't as high as I'd hoped.

No more excuses for going to the same restaurant again, missing the one concert I wanted to see, or enduring another evening of takeout and rereading *The Catcher in the Rye* when a city of entertainment options awaits me...The Seattle Sidewalk city guide (published by you-know-who) is now available free on the Web and as a featured offering on MSN. Supercool! And we'll have another ten to fifteen other Sidewalk guides launched in key cities by the end of the year! Into orbit! This is the killer application the Web's been waiting for...City guides will make the Internet truly relevant to Joe Schmoe: a combination of yellow pages, movie guide, entertainment section, classified ads, restaurant reviews, and community bulletin board. Always up to date and easy to find. And guess whose idea it was? MINE! Yeaaaahhhhh!

FRIDAY, APRIL 4

More evidence of my true visionary status dropped on my desk today. A report by Forrester Research says that the revenue from Internet gameplay will soar during the next five years to over $1.5 billion! And I've already set up our Gaming Zone! And what's more, I've done a cool deal with Hasbro for some wicked, wicked games...Look out for new Internet versions of Monopoly...Risk...Battleship...Yahtzee...and Scrabble...Yeaahhhh! The kids out there are clamoring for this kind of stuff. Honest.

I noticed that today was the anniversary of Martin Luther King's death, twenty-nine years ago. I know he didn't invent BASIC or Windows or the Internet, but in his own way he was a pretty important guy.

The huge success of the Spice Girls as a direct result of my influential support has not gone unnoticed! E-mail from the girls!

> To: BillG
> From: MelB
> Bill honey, you're really nice 'n' spicy, just like the five of us...but we really wannabe just like you. Maybe we can zig-a-zig-ahh sometime?

This is SO exciting! I gotta respond QUICK! But first...I comb my hair (and put on my cool Tom Cruise shades!) before sending the e-mail—hoping to appear attractive...

> Hi! MelB...Baybeeeeee...
> Mel—is this REALLY you? You're my favorite! You're the best looking, most talented Spice Girl. You should go solo! Wow! This is SO cool! Please send me your autograph by e-mail! Wanna talk about the Internet with ME?!!!!!!!!!
> Regards, Spicy Bill G.

Gee, I hope I didn't sound TOO eager. I always try to play it cool...

SUNDAY, APRIL 6

DAYLIGHT SAVING TIME BEGINS

Went to Barnes & Noble in my search of…enlightenment, education, entertainment, and…NEW BOOKS ABOUT ME! Bingo! It's *Deeper* by John Seabrook. He's the guy that wrote about me in the *New Yorker* a couple of years back, and now he's turned that article into a full-length book. Still, endlessly recycling (or "repurposing" as we call it in the digital biz) old material is a good thing. It certainly hasn't done Visual Basic—the ultimate language, right?—any harm.

BTW it's pretty good for the first half or so—which is about ME!—but goes downhill rapidly after that…he starts discussing the Well and His Wife and His Mac and other dull stuff…

Someone once said to me, "Bill, what do you think of free software?" and I said, "It's great. I like the idea of free hardware, too." Boy, I'm such a funny guy.

"Keep your feet on the ground and keep reachin' for the stars."

CASEY KASEM

MONDAY, APRIL 7

Of course, it is possible that free hardware is getting ever closer. I mean, it's all about the market-share metric, and some guys think that dumb, set-top boxes are the way forward. Ad revenue plus subscriptions would effectively make them FREE. But, in the end, I'd guess that people will want more power, flexibility...and the ability to CREATE rather than just digest. You know, there's absolutely no way that a box that provides just passive entertainment could ever get into more than about 5% of American homes.

Still, just to be on the safe side...I bought WebTV. And only $425 million! It's a new era in computing, entertainment, and communications—and underscores our strategy of delivering to consumers the benefits of the Internet together with emerging forms of digital broadcasting. Windows is gonna be EVERYWHERE! Rock 'n' roll!

I just heard that the Spice Girls have sold over 10 million copies of their supercool #1 hit album *Spice*...All thanks to me! Only another 50 million copies or so before they catch up with Windows—MY supercool #1 hit operating system.

TUESDAY, APRIL 8

Oh, my... WinHEC—the world's largest hardware developers' conference...Another show, another keynote speech...Am I famous, or what? (Trick question: I am WAY famous.)

I have to admit that Melinda's been giving me a hard time lately—ever since I made that comment about chicks and software. (Well. It's true. Chicks CAN'T do software companies. It's a biological thing, OK?) And now I've gotten a response from that software chick over at Marimba...(And it IS a stupid name, OK?)

> Bill,
> Maybe you should liven your dull Microsoft site up with some groovy Castanet stuff...proof that software by chicks is better than software by guys. And check out the sexy picture of me over at my site. It'll make you zig-a-zig-ohhh...
> Kim Polecat, Marimba

I'll admit the photo's pretty good...For a software chick, Spicy KimP ain't bad! She might even be worth employing after Castanet becomes one of the victims in the shakeout of Internet push technology...

And $2 million, from the *National Enquirer,* for the exclusive North American rights to ten photographs of Michael's baby boy, Prince Michael Jackson Jr. If only they'd asked me! I'd have taken eleven pictures of Princess Jennifer Katharine Gates for only $1.9 million! (Or less. After all, I always price for maximum market share. Who knows? The celebrity baby picture segment may one day be an important strategic market.)

WEDNESDAY, APRIL 9

An enormous amount is written about where technology is taking us. Some of the writing is knowledgeable, but a lot of it is ill informed, random, or contradictory. Or just plain dumb. So, it's always good to get a break from the serious business of competitor crushing with some lighthearted reading...Like *Forbes,* and their article on Corel... "Michael Cowpland has amassed a confederation of beaten armies and declared war on Bill Gates. Will revenge be theirs?" Help me! Help me! Who are these guys kidding? Beat me? With what? WordPerfect Office Suite? Right. Java Office? Yeah, sure. Cowpland? Just another loser with big dreams...

THURSDAY, APRIL 10

Now, THIS is what I call great writing...It's my favorite quote of the week..."Microsoft's Internet Explorer is good software. Really good. Way better than Netscape..." Said Jeffrey Veen, Interface Director for *HotWired.* See? I've been telling everyone this all along. *Hasta la vista,* Marc! The browser wars are definitely over. (Thanks, Jeffrey. At least, that's what I thought he said....Maybe it was wishful thinking.)

Finally! Some decent games for the Gaming Zone...I've been hyping Scrabble, Monopoly, and bridge, but I have to admit it's kinda tough. I mean, they're not exactly Doom, right? But now I've done a supercool deal with LucasArts for their Star Wars games. (I can finally forget that Romero guy. Doom wasn't THAT good, anyway.)

So...What do you get if you cross CompuServe with AOL? An on-line service with 14 million losers!

FRIDAY, APRIL 11

Melinda's decided to let me in on her Top Ten Rejection Lines Given by Women (and what they actually mean). Maybe it's still funny to her, but I'm kinda sensitive about this stuff...

1. I've got a boyfriend. (You're a loser.)

2. There's a slight difference in our ages. (I don't want to sleep with my dad.)

3. I'm not attracted to you in THAT way. (You're a nerd.)

4. My life is too complicated right now. (I don't want you spending the whole night in case you hear phone calls from all the other guys I'm seeing.)

5. I think of you as a brother. (You remind me of that inbred banjo-playing geek in *Deliverance*.)

6. I don't date men where I work. (I wouldn't date you if you were the only man in the

same solar system, much less the same building. And you're not my boss, so there's no chance of getting a promotion out of it.)

7. Our lifestyles aren't compatible. (You're not rich enough for me.)

8. It's not you, it's me. (It's you.)

9. I'm concentrating on my career. (Even something as boring and unfulfilling as my job is better than dating you.)

10. Let's be friends. (I want you to stay around so I can tell you in excruciating detail about all the other men I meet and have sex with.)

SATURDAY, APRIL 12

As Melinda has shared her Top Ten, it's only fair that I give the male equivalent. Of course, these days I'm a happily married man, and dating is a thing of the past. But I think I can still remember my super-useful Top Ten Kiss-Off Lines (and what they REALLY mean)...

1. I've got a girlfriend. (You're ugly.)

2. There's a slight difference in our ages. (You're ugly.)

3. I'm not attracted to you in THAT way. (You're REALLY ugly.)

4. My life is way too complicated right now. (You're ugly.)

5. I think of you as a sister. (You're way ugly.)

6. I don't date women where I work. (You're ugly.)

7. Our lifestyles aren't compatible. (You're ugly.)

8. It's not you, it's me. (You're ugly.)

9. I'm concentrating on Microsoft. (You're ugly.)

10. Let's be friends. (Man! Are you ugly!)

SUNDAY, APRIL 13

Melinda was very philosophical at breakfast today...She wants to know how I can live with myself after ruthlessly crushing my competitors. "You know," I said, "I'm healthy, I'm sane, I'm happy, I'm rich." I guess that about sums it up...

Today was the London Marathon in sunny England (that poor little country with just five TV channels!). And Microsoft's very own David Svendsen took part. Cool. But less time on the training please, and more time on beefing up those U.K. sales. OK? Slacker...

And today, I decided to invent...The Network Computer...The NC's gonna be SO cool...I think

I'll call it a "Windows Terminal" and it'll run Windows NC...Yeaaahhhhhh!

"Electronic mail is an early harbinger of the infosphere."

BILL GATES

MONDAY, APRIL 14

It looks like Ellison really does want to be president of two big thingies...He's still talking about taking over Apple, helped by his buddy, Saudi billionaire (nowhere close to 30 billion!) Prince Al-Waleed bin Talal, who disclosed that he had already purchased more than 5% of the company. Don't you have any work to do, Larry?

And congratulations to Tiger Woods for winning the Masters at twenty-one...I think I'd made my first billion by twenty-one...But, hey, you gotta start somewhere, right?

TUESDAY, APRIL 15

Rupert Murdoch's finally slowing down over at News Corporation...He's promoted his kid, Lachlan, to big corporate cheese...This could be the break I need in my push into the content biz...And Lachlan's twenty-five already, so he's pretty old. I figure I'll have Jennifer groomed for stardom by...say, six or so. She should be ready to take over a little division—like Corbis—by then. That's my girl! She's the ONLY chick who COULD do a software company...

And I see that America Online is now claiming 9 million members. Made-up-number alert!

WEDNESDAY, APRIL 16

Kinsley, over at *Slate,* is finally taking my "advice." I TOLD him that he'd have to cover naked chicks and rock 'n' roll to get the readers...And, in the latest issue, he features Courtney Hole, of Love. (Or is it Courtney Love, of Hole? Whatever.) That's my boy.

And guess who e-mailed me today?

From: Philippe K, Starfish Software

I read a funny anecdote on the Net. Someone was saying that you are amazingly smart, getting everyone to believe that it's okay to keep all that money because you "will" give it all away later...Very smart. Or is it very sad?

Good to see you're still in business, Philippe. It's a nice little company. You're right—I am way richer than you, and I am amazingly smart. And I WILL give it all away later. Honest.

THURSDAY, APRIL 17

At last! I finally crashed through the $30 billion mark on my net worth, on my announcement of stellar quarterly revenue and earnings. Wow! Over 8 million Office licenses helped generate record revenues. (And we're selling a license every SECOND! Cooool! So...maybe it's more like "there's SIXTY born every minute"...) It MUST be time for a Big Billy Bonus now!

FRIDAY, APRIL 18

The upside of my newfound wealth is that I can finally afford to buy...the little Hawaiian island of Lanai (Ah! Fond memories of my honeymoon...), which is, I hear, for sale. I'm sure Melinda would really appreciate it. I could build my own theme park...Yeahhh! The FIRST computer theme park... Windows World! Microland! Or (too cool!) Billywood! A place for the cyberjunkies of the world to converge and enjoy such supercool rides as SOFTWARE Pirates of the Caribbean...The Tunnel of I LOVE DOS...Free DOWNLOAD Fall...It's MY Small World...BILL's Internet Express...GATES Mountain...and the It Don't MATTER When It's Ready 'Cause I'll Just Change the Year in the Software Name HORN...Awesome! Yeeaaaahhhhh!

The downside of my newfound wealth is that my Gap khakis no longer fit properly. I have to get my Seattle tailor to make more of those too cool, handmade ones...with an extra-large wallet pocket. Man! Life is hard!

And that Kim Polese...Now she's being featured in *Time*! One of the twenty-five Most Influential Americans? Give me a BREAK! Look, Castanet ain't that exciting! (Active Desktop's gonna be WAY cooler...And Marimba's STILL a stupid name.) The Web's IT Girl? Oh, yeah...right! And another thing...HOW CAN YOU LEAVE *ME* OUT? YOU GUYS ARE JUST SO UNBELIEVABLY RANDOM. CANCEL MY SUBSCRIPTION. LIKE NOW. OK? JEEZ...RANDOM, RANDOM, *RANDOM*...

Jennifer's been real busy and come up with her Top Ten In-the-News Celebrity Babies (after her, that is). Man, she's so smart! That's my girl!

1. **Princess Jennifer Katharine Gates** (OK, she couldn't resist.)

2. **Prince Michael Jackson Jr.** (Wacko daddo.)

3. **Lola Montessori** (That's Madonna's kid, stupid!)

4. **Brandon Anderson Lee** (Cute mom. With her own Web page. Or three.)

5. Ummm...

6. **Michael Dell's twins** (An industry connection!)

7. **Baby Spice** (Cooool!)

8. Er...There aren't any more...

9. Wait! **The former baby of the Artist Formerly Known as Prince...**

10. Now, there DEFINITELY aren't any more...

"It is a wise father that knows his own child." WILLIAM SHAKESPEARE

MONDAY, APRIL 21

PATRIOTS' DAY
(MASSACHUSETTS AND MAINE)

Check out the latest Zona Research survey I commissioned on Customer Satisfaction with Educational Aids...(I decided to select a typically representative sample: Baby Jennifer.)

Princess Jennifer Satisfaction Rating
with Educational Aids

Lion King (Walt Disney, video)	95.9%
Barney the Dinosaur (Microsoft, toy-type thing)	4.0%
Molecular Biology of the Gene (Watson, book)	0.1%

Hmmm...I think Melinda's been undermining my educational efforts by allowing Jennifer access to the VCR. I keep telling her that TV is a decadent, mind-sapping self-indulgence (apart from *Seinfeld* and *Friends,* of course). If I wasn't out all day slaving to put food on the table, this survey would have been totally different...

TUESDAY, APRIL 22

FIRST DAY OF PASSOVER

Picture this... I've got an orchard that yields a crop, of say, 100 apples a year. (It's a small orchard, but, for this example, small is OK.) I need to make at least $100 to feed my loving wife and delightful daughter (who, for privacy reasons, shall remain nameless). Let's say you come to me and you want to buy just one apple. I'll charge you $2. But if you came to me and wanted to have 50 apples, I'd maybe only charge you $1.50 each. And if you wanted the whole crop, you could maybe bargain me down to $1.25 or less. It's called economy of scale...the law of the free-market economy. (Of course, if I had a major apple orchard competitor then my apples are free. Forever. But that's another story.)

So, if a Top Five PC builder comes to me with an order for a few trillion units of MS Office, he gets a decent bulk-buy discount and can buy the product for, say, $20 per unit. But if you're Mr. No-Name-San trying to buy a handful of units to bundle with your shoddy, Far Eastern clone machines, you're gonna have to pay the full $200 a pop. It's how the world works. It's not my fault.

So stick that where the sun don't shine, Mr. European Community, and crawl back to Brussels, or Paris, or wherever it is you come from. It's called VOLUME DISCOUNT.

WEDNESDAY, APRIL 23

SECRETARIES' DAY

Some people have been questioning (And if they're so smart how come they aren't worth $30 billion? Huh? Now that's what I call a question.) the value of my strategic WebTV acquisition...Look guys, it's simple...An analysis of U.S. households gives the following penetrations: PCs at 30%, TVs at 98%. OK? I gotta cover all the form factors. And that's an awful lot of copies of Windows CE. Coooool!

This network computer idea is just so stoooopid! Networks will be overloaded if PCs go diskless. The cost of the server will go up, a lot more than the cost of the disks would. Well, that's just my humble opinion. And if I am proved wrong (which, of course, I won't be), at least I've got the NetPC in reserve.

And if they'd done it right, this is what the *Time* Top Ten Most Influential Americans (after me, that is!) would have looked like...

1. **Bill Gates.** (Sorry. I just couldn't help myself, OK?)

2. **Warren Buffett.** He's rich, he's smart, he's my pal.

3. **Paul Allen.** He's rich, he's smart, he's my pal.

4. **Steve Ballmer.** The General Patton of software.

5. **Bill #2.** Clinton, that is. Not rich, but not to be underestimated . . . He could still order a preemptive strike on Microsoft Campus.

6. **Melinda French Gates.** The power behind the throne…A few days of the silent treatment, and boy does she have some influence.

7. **Nathan Myhrvold.** A technical visionary, a book author, a barbecue expert. Is there no end to his talents? (And influence, of course.)

8. **Princess Jennifer Katharine Gates.** Still young, but she has the ear of the world's richest man. That's my girl!

8. **Larry Ellison.** Whatever he says, I do the opposite. Works every time.

10. **My pop.** I'd say he was pretty influential. Especially now that he has control of the magnificently endowed Bill-Gates-Can't-Be-All- That-Bad-If-He's-Giving-Away-All-This-Money Fund…

SATURDAY, APRIL 26

PRINCESS JENNIFER GATES DAY

Jennifer is one year old today…Happy Birthday, Jennifer. Daddy loves you! I got her a copy of our brand new and totally awesome "The Magic School Bus Explores the Rainforest." Cool! God bless free evaluation software! (And God bless America, too!)

SUNDAY, APRIL 27

ORTHODOX EASTER

The *Slate* 60 Quarterly Update of supernice people giving away lots of money is out. And I've zoomed up to #7 with a supergenerous $10 million donation to Lakeside School. (Hey, I only made a paltry $10 billion in stock appreciation during the last six months.)

The charity Top Ten is one where I used to think that you DIDN'T want to be top...But now I'm not so sure...Allen's at #5 with $15 million—and I'm not going to let him beat me at ANYTHING!

On the other hand, having all this money means I'm a potentially huge philanthropist—so the new magazine, *American Benefactor,* features me on the cover. Thanks, guys! I'll give it all away later...honest.

"The Library of Congress is a Dumpster full of atoms."

NICHOLAS NEGROPONTE

MONDAY, APRIL 28

Today I was in sunny Detroit for a press conference to announce that Microsoft had donated $1.5 million in software and financial aid to Focus:HOPE.

I like to do what I can for charity...I just want to know how we can get *Slate* to add the Microsoft donations to mine, so that I beat Paul Allen in the Top Ten Givers List. I mean, that's fair, right? It's sort of my money anyway...

Joseph Carter, a BS candidate at Focus:HOPE's Center for Advanced Technologies, made a presentation: "Bill, you are so huge. So really, really huge. And we're so small. So very, very small. Insignificant, in fact. We are not worthy. We are not worthy. Let me lick your shoes clean..."

Of course, that's not what he REALLY said. But, hey, whatever...That's what he SHOULD have said. Thanks, Joe! (My shoes are REALLY shiny now.)

TUESDAY, APRIL 29

Interesting developments over at Citibank, which has promoted this Campbell dude to be in charge of...well, nearly everything, in fact. They reckon they can market the bank as a consumer brand like P&G, Nike, Gillette, and Philip Morris. Which, of course, is what I want to do with Microsoft. I want to reinforce the Microsoft brand and find opportunities to cross-sell products over the complete range of our distribution systems. It's all about global consumer branding. And global consumer domination. I can do that.

Compiled my list of favorite exercises. Here's my Top Ten:

1. **The Super-Efficient Push-Up**™.

2. **Coding twenty-nine hours straight.** Yeah.

3. **Trampolining.**

4. **Co-ed naked Twister.** (With Melinda, of course.)

5. **Shopping at the Gap.**

6. **Getting it on with M.** (Closely related to #4, I guess.)

7. **Armchair jumping.**

8. **World domination.** (While wearing wrist weights.)

9. **My rocking thing.**

10. **The regular push-up.**

WEDNESDAY, APRIL 30

You know, it's just so frustrating...sometimes I think the only way to do it right is to do it myself. (And that's true. But, hey, even I can't do everything.) These builders are just so incompetent. Will they ever finish my little love nest? Look, it's not like Melinda and I ask for many changes...they're just a few teeny-weeny adjustments here and there. Nothing that should affect the schedule...if the work wasn't being done by the building world's equivalent of

Apple. And worst of all, it means that my planned tête-á-tête with a bunch of industry CEOs and some government leaders can't take place there. Instead we're going to slum it down at the Four Seasons. (Although that does save me having to program over 100 different music and video preferences in my downstairs bathroom. Phew!)

THURSDAY, MAY 1

Will my problems never end? I was cruising the Net today looking for any Bill-based material and what did I find? An UNOFFICIAL Bill Gates Diary...And a pretty pathetic attempt it is too. It sounds nothing like me. I'm just so annoyed. Furious, in fact. I mean, I don't mind the odd Bill tribute and, of course, I've got a great sense of humor, but...

Big news from the U.K. (that sad, strange little country with only five TV channels) is their presidential election...Tony Blair takes it in a landslide. Well done, Tony! And don't forget: U.K. schools need more Microsoft software!

Larry announced that he won't be taking over Apple. What a surprise! I knew the big wimp was full of hot air.

FRIDAY, MAY 2

Hot date with Melinda! Yeaaahhhhh! Took her to see the new box office smash *Volcano*...It was great for me, but she said that the volcano erupted far too soon. Is she trying to tell me something?

SATURDAY, MAY 3

Kasparov vs. IBM Deep Blue...Start

of the six-game, $1.1 million challenge. Last year, GaryK beat the machine 4–2. So, what's gonna happen this year? Of course, it's slightly disappointing not to be taking part myself, because I am a GREAT chess player (I'm sure PaulA agrees.) If I hadn't chosen to dominate the computer biz and the biggest personal fortune contest, I'd have been world champion. (Or a Nobel Prize–winning physicist. Damn! So many choices!)

I bet I could write a better chess-playing program over the weekend in Excel Macros. (That's how cool I am.) Then, next year...Kasparov vs. Microsoft Big Bill...

SUNDAY, MAY 4

I keep getting asked by my friends, family, and various supermodels: "What's the ideal PC,

Bill?" Dumb question. But I like to think I'm a constructive, helpful guy, so here's my recommended specification...(Remember, it doesn't matter how good the PC is, or how much you spend...thanks to Moore's Law, as soon as you carry it out of the shop it turns into an eight-track tape player.)

1. **Pentium 300 with MMX** (From my buddy Andy.)

2. **40 Mb of RAM**

3. **4.5 Gb hard drive**

4. **20x CD-ROM**

5. **LOUD** speakers

6. **56K modem**

7. **Microsoft Mouse**

8. **Microsoft Natural Keyboard**

9. **Microsoft Joy Stick**

10. **Microsoft MS-DOS**

11. **Microsoft Windows**

12. **Microsoft Office**

13. **Microsoft Encarta**

14. **Microsoft Money**

15. **Microsoft Internet Explorer** (This one's free, OK?)

16. **Microsoft Games Pack** (Way better than Doom. Honest.)

17. **Subscription to MSN** (Does NOT suck!)

18. **Microsoft Flight Simulator**

19. **Microsoft Bob** (Just kidding!)

20. **Microsoft Barney the Dinosaur** (Sitting cutely on the top of your monitor.)

"Where do you want to go today?" MICROSOFT

MONDAY, MAY 5

Melinda agrees. This "Bill Diary" stuff goes way too far. It's obviously written by a pathetic loser—probably the president of a competing software company with a grudge to bear because he didn't invent DOS, BASIC, Windows, or the Internet. It has to stop. I'm not the most powerful guy on the planet for nothing. Lawyers at dawn.

I can't believe it! Can't anyone talk some sense into Paul Allen over this Ticketmaster thing? How can he sue us? Microsoft is his company too! And over what? Just because our Seattle Sidewalk site links to his Ticketmaster site...This has to be the stupidest thing I've ever heard.

TUESDAY, MAY 6

Gary, Gary, Gary... Only managing a 2–2
draw (so far) with a machine? What are you doing?
Surely you know by now that once you open up the
queen's side in the Ruy Lopez (Andreessen Variation)
you have to go in for the kill. I could have done better!
Drop by my house sometime and I'll give you a few
tips. Oh...it's not finished yet. Okay, when it's FIN-
ISHED drop by...Are you LISTENING, builder men?

Hmmmm...Having a few problems with the im-
plementation of Microsoft Big Bill...Excel Macros?
That's just the stupidest thing I've ever heard. Visual
Basic's more like it. Now that's what I call a REAL
programming language...

WEDNESDAY, MAY 7

I'm convinced that Microsoft is going to dom-
inate the future. And not just because we're smart.
(Although we are. An organization with a billion IQ
points. And lots of them are mine!) It's because of the
vision thing. We have a STRATEGY. You see, new
wealth is always the result of industry revolution.
And industry revolution is the result of strategic innovation. Our capability for strategic innovation is
our key competitive edge. And that's a result of our
passion: our passion for excellence...our passion for
new products...our passion for more money...And

because we promote genetic diversity within the organization. We don't want an organization built on a hierarchy of experience. We want an organization built on a hierarchy of imagination. More youth, more creative types, more eccentrics to go with our technologists: a broad-based creative synergy.

And as long as they all think I'm God, we'll get along just fine.

THURSDAY, MAY 8

Who could get the Top 100 CEOs (and one world leader, if Al Gore counts) in one room to listen to him speak? (And have grown men fighting to get invited!) Me! I'm the clever Bill! But we should have had more chicks...I didn't see spicy KimP anywhere...Maybe I should have arranged for the Top 100 Women CEOs...Or the Top 100 Supermodels...And how the Internet is going to shape their futures...With some "hands-on" training from yours truly...Yeaaaahhhhhh! Maybe next year!

Took them to dinner at my place. At least the banqueting room is finished!

FRIDAY, MAY 9

Now I have another valuable company...Teledesic, my little "Internet in the sky" venture with my buddy Craig McCaw, is joining forces with Boeing. Boeing is taking a 10% stake for $100 million, giving the company a $1 billion valuation. I know it's not Microsoft, but for a start-up that's pretty good.

And a global satellite network delivering Microsoft content to WebTV boxes everywhere. That looks pretty good, too. Am I cool or what? (Do you honestly need me to tell you the answer? It's a trick question! I am WAY, WAY COOL!)

SATURDAY, MAY 10

Wow! Check out MSFT! Microsoft stock is just unstoppable. To infinity and beyond! Hmmmm... Where have I heard that before?

With the latest rise, I made a cool $5 billion in the last month! Yeaaahhhhh! And I worked really hard for it too! Hands up, everyone who made less than $20,000...Feel bad? Feel inadequate? Feel poor? Yup, you are a LOSER. Hee, hee, hee...

SUNDAY, MAY 11

MOTHER'S DAY

Helped Jennifer make a Mother's Day card for Melinda using Microsoft Greetings. What a great product! What a great company!

Went down to Barnes & Noble for my regular check on important new releases. You know, new books about Visual Basic...the latest from Andy Grove...yet another Tom Peters book on Excellence...NOT! I want more books about ME! The way I figure it, the number of books about any one person should be directly proportional to their net worth...Which means I'm still owed another 320 biographies, and another 19,300 magazine articles. Get writing, guys! I'm a really interesting person...

"Make it so, Number One."

JEAN-LUC PICARD

MONDAY, MAY 12

Poor old GaryK. Losing against a machine. (Demand a rematch, chess dude!) Deep Blue takes the series 3 to 2—the first victory for machine against man. Gary threw a little temper tantrum at the end. He looked kinda upset about the whole thing . . . I'd like to say I know how he feels. But I've never lost at anything in my WHOLE LIFE. Welcome to the world of LOSERS, Gary. Hee, hee, hee.

TUESDAY, MAY 13

Yeaaaaahhhhhh! I've been featured in *Wired* again! Thanks guys! And in your honor, here's my very own Tired/Wired list...

101

Over Tired	Way Wired
Mike and the Mechanics	Spice Girls
OS 8	Windows 98
Poverty	$40 billion personal fortunes
NC	Pentium 300 w/64mb RAM, 4.5gb drive, multi-media & Windows 95
Chicks running software companies	Chicks!
TV	WebTV
Suits	Gap Khakis
Anything by Netscape	IE4
Larry Ellison	Me!!!!!!!!

WEDNESDAY, MAY 14

Jeez! All I do is invite a few guys over to my new pad to dialog, and the papers (and those grrrl Web sites) are now full of how I'm antiwomen. And it's just not true. I think chicks are cool. Way cool. They just can't run a software business. Or any other big business. They make GREAT hairdressers, massage therapists, supermodels...and mothers. Melinda's just so much happier and fulfilled now that she can stay home all day looking after Baby Jennifer. They may SAY that their career at Microsoft is the most important thing, but you KNOW that they'll give it up for the first multibillionaire that asks them.

THURSDAY, MAY 15

Melinda tried to ban me from the house for being a sexist pig! Chicks? Don't you just love 'em? We'll see who's laughing when I upgrade to new, improved Wife 98! Ha!

What about Microsoft Show Tunes? Classics like "If I Were a Rich Man..." This speaks to ME...

FRIDAY, MAY 16

Or, "If I Ruled the World..." But, I do...

SATURDAY, MAY 17

ARMED FORCES DAY

I got this e-mail message today from one of my fans. Everybody loves me!

> From: Mark J.
> To: Happenin' Bill G.
> You are *the best*!
> The purpose of this e-mail is to tell you that you're my all-time, number-one, hands-down, no-questions-asked HERO! Compared to you I'm just a zero!

You're so right! I am the best. (I must be—I'm the richest.) And you're just a zero! But at least you're man enough to admit it—unlike Larry, Marc, Steve, and all those other industry losers...

SUNDAY, MAY 18

My all-time favorite singing stars (apart from the Spice Girls) are the superhip Bee Gees. They are SO cool! I've been a huge fan since *Saturday Night Fever*. And I've always wanted to have my hair like that...but Melinda won't let me. Huh! What does she know about the fab world of groovy sounds?

With the incredible rise of the Internet, my electronic rights to the world's greatest art should be pretty useful. And it won't be a monopoly! Microsoft will own the software, and I'll own the content! But there's still a long way to go. Here's my Top Ten List of Things I Don't Own Electronic Rights To...(Yet)

1. Every *Star Trek* episode
2. Every *Star Trek TNG* episode
3. Every Beatles song
4. Every Michael Jackson song
5. Elvis
6. Ansel Adams
7. *The Catcher in the Rye*
8. *The X-Files*
9. NASA
10. The Bible (Old & New Testaments)

"Bill Gates is Elvis." DAVE BARRY

MONDAY, MAY 19

VICTORIA DAY (CANADA)

A new survey shows that over twenty million Americans find the Internet indispensable. Good thing I invented it then, huh?

Today was exciting. I got some more babe-mail! Yeaaaahhhhhh!

Dear Bill:

I have long been an extreme admirer of yours and would just simply LOVE to see personal photos of you, and since I am a really hot babe, I would LOVE IT MORE if those photos were just the slightest bit naughty. Your haircut is such a turn-on, maybe you could put a photo of the comb you use on-line. Wow, I am already hot for it!

Signed, Nina,
rich, hot, smart babe who boffs
only nerds in San Francisco

Exciting, eh? Although I have to be careful in case it's Larry Ellison or Steve Jobs luring me into an indiscretion...

TUESDAY, MAY 20

So I decided to reply:

Hi, Nina:

Of course, that's only natural. And it's not just my body that's impressive—I have a big, ahem, IQ too. I find that most women find a powerful intellect to be a major turn-on. Surprisingly, despite what people say, money seems a relatively minor concern. I'm glad—I believe that a woman should want me for MYSELF.

Regards, Bill G.

Maybe she's really cute, like Melinda. Ha, ha.

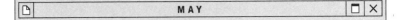

As you all know, in my humble opinion, a good market share is anything over 55%. And a good Microsoft market share is anything over 85%. So here's a question for young Marc down at Netscape HQ...When and why is 35% a GREAT market share? Yup, you've guessed it! When it's up from 5% (against a dominant 95% market leader) in just six months...and with that kind of growth, parity (and then leadership, of course) can't be far away! LOSER!

And with their clear failure to maintain their dominant market position, it's no surprise that their stock is collapsing faster than...than, er, well, a really fast collapsing thing...With performance like that, it's only fair that Barksdale has agreed to take a pay cut to $1 a year. I'm not even sure I'd pay him that dollar. LOSER!

Oops. I was a bit slow hitting on Tea Leoni, the babe from *As the World Turns*...I'm sure she would have LOVED to talk about the Internet with me, but now she's gone and married Scully from *The X-Files*. Or is Mulder? Whatever! Either way, he's not as good looking (or rich) as me. Beats me what she sees in a guy who hasn't invented a single computer product of any significance.

Millions of people around the world breathed a collective sigh of relief when a crazed psycho Apple Mac fanatic was arrested before he could carry out his fiendish plot to extort money and/or kill the world's greatest visionary (that's me!). Luckily, my security people had it all covered right from the start. And I knew he was a loser when I read his e-mail death threats. A sad, strange little man.

And $5 million? Get real, loser! I'm the richest man in the world. Were you trying to nickel and dime me to death? Relax everyone! I'm still here. (And I've still got all my money. Phew!)

Hey! Dr. Pop at the Pop Desk! It's official! My protégés, the Spice Girls, are officially the biggest chick group in America (and the world). My job is done. Now I need to look for the Next Insanely Great Thing...And I think I know who it is...You won't have heard of her yet (because, as usual, I'm way ahead of you), but this new chick Jenny McCarthy is gonna be a big star. She's got looks, talent, and great breasts. With my help, she might just make it. Her own TV show? A Web site dedicated to her? Being a centerfold? Give me a call, Jenny, and I'll see what I can do for you...

My babe-mail correspondence continues with:

Nina:
If you have a small GIF you can e-mail, I might enjoy that. (If you really are a "hot, smart, rich babe.") You know, boffing nerds is really out. Unless they own Microsoft...

Regards, Bill G.

I figure there's no harm in asking, right?

SUNDAY, MAY 25

If these random, random, contractors can't finish the house in time, I'm obviously going to have to do some of the work myself. I headed down to Home Depot to get started...I really really wanna wanna can a paint, ahhhh...

No new books about me down at Barnes & Noble. Instead I reread my copy of the awesome *Brief History of Time.* I noticed from the sleeve photo that Stephen Hawking has a really cool haircut. If I could have a snazzy do like that I'd be a total babe magnet...I'd be a black hole: so attractive that no chick could escape my gravity. Yeaaaahhhhhh!

"Do, or do not.
There is no try."

YODA *(THE EMPIRE STRIKES BACK)*

MONDAY, MAY 26

MEMORIAL DAY

Those that know me, know that I like to live life on the edge...So now I'm Doin' the Dew. Radical! Duuuuuuuude! I can jump over my desk from a standing start. I bet Marc Andreessen can't do that. These young kids today just don't have what it takes to succeed in the corporate world.

Wow! Nina responds. Usually they don't believe it's me!

Bill:
Really do wish I had a small GIF to send you but maybe you could find one of Cindy Crawford 'cause that is who I really look like.

Boffing RICH nerds NEVER goes out of current fashion.

Nina.

And she looks like Cindy!! Yeeeaaaahhhh!!!

TUESDAY, MAY 27

It's interesting to see how the big fear of Microsoft has died down. When we were just dominating the operating system (DOS and Windows) and productivity software market (with the best word processor, spreadsheet, and database) there was big-time paranoia and anti-MS sentiments. Now that we're poised to dominate PCs, TVs, palmtops, broadband Internet delivery via Teledesic's satellite network—and leveraging a whole bunch of our MSN and MSNBC content...well, in comparison, the silence is deafening. But, hey, why should I complain?

Maybe everyone has given up fighting the inevitable. I mean, resistance IS futile. And with our stock still surging upward, Microsoft is now the third largest (market cap) company in the world. Only Coke and General Electric are stopping us from assuming our rightful place. Hey! That big #1 spot won't be long now! Can there be any doubt about who's the most powerful man on the planet? (Hint: he's the richest! Another hint: it's ME, dummy!)

WEDNESDAY, MAY 28

I have to come up with some good competitive strategies for hitting that #1 spot...Hmmmm... Maybe Melinda's right...We'll put out our new product range of "Simply Interactive" household appliances...When they hit the market, nobody will want that old-fashioned junk that GE sells! (I wonder if preannouncements work as well in the consumer market as they do in the software biz?) Maybe I should rethink our MSNBC joint venture? And Coke? I'm switching our free soda policy to a free Pepsi policy! (And telling Warren to stop buying their stock!) At least I can keep on Doin' the Dew...It's a PepsiCo product!

Here's my list of the Top Ten Borland Employees I'd Like to Steal...

1. Anders Hejlsberg

2. Delbert Yocam

3. Uh, is there anyone left? Turn the lights off on your way out, Delbert.

4. Nah...I'm just kidding! OK? Trust me! I would NEVER, EVER, EVER try to damage another company by soliciting all their good employees.

5. Double your salary! Big signing bonus! Stock options that go UP in value! Work on products that actually sell! Free Pepsi! Call me NOW!

THURSDAY, MAY 29

Hey! Took in a movie with my baby...Melinda and I went to see *The Lost World*, Spielberg's follow-up to *Jurassic Park*. Cool effects. Well done, Steve!

I want to be a Certified Microsoft Office User, too! I'm really good—I even use PIVOT TABLES! (And being CMOU-qualified could be just the edge I need when I go looking for my next job...)

Man! It's been a busy few weeks for lawsuits! Me and Andy have been comparing notes to see if any of these pesky little things have any merit—or if any of the teeny little companies involved have enough money to keep fighting! Andy's having fun with Cyrix and Digital over alleged patent infringements, while I'm still trying to get Paul and Ticketmaster to see sense. (Paul's just sold his Ticketmaster stake to the Home Shopping Network...Barry Diller's a pal of mine—I think I can make HIM see things my way.) And, in the latest, I'm fighting off the mighty (ha, ha!) Borland. They claim we're stealing their staff. As if! It's not my fault that all those Borland (and Apple!) employees want a real job with a real company! (And get stock options that go UP in value! And a signing bonus! And free Pepsi! Call me NOW!)

But wait a minute... That signing bonus should be realistic. Who authorized a $3 million signing bonus for Anders Hejlsberg? It couldn't have been me. I bet it was Nathan "Well, It's Not My Money" Myhrvold. I mean, the guy's just a programmer! A Delphi programmer! He probably doesn't even know the first thing about Visual Basic!

113

And a $200,000 salary? That's nearly as much as me! What's going on around here? It wasn't like this in the early days when I was running the HR department, too.

More horrific, vindictive stuff on the Web...A picture of Melinda from her high school yearbook, and a claim (unsubstantiated, of course) that she's had a nose job. I can tell you that Melinda is all natural. And besides, money spent on plastic surgery is way too inefficient when you can use it to crush a couple of (small) competitors instead.

On the other hand, maybe a teeny $6,000 investment would be worthwhile...Then Melinda could have a Jenny McCarthy–style chest. Yeaaaaahhhhhh!

"There's more to life than e-mail." NICHOLAS NEGROPONTE

Stop the builders right now! I've just heard that Larry's building a *$40 million* home—a replica of a sixteenth-century samurai village—on twenty-three acres of land near San Francisco. It's

like, Zen and the Art of Really Big House Building...
I bet Larry's hoping to be featured in *Architectural
Digest* (and *Koi Breeder's Monthly*). More signifi-
cantly, that's nearly as much as my little house. No
way! Add a Koi pond...Add a Moon Pavilion...
Make those gold-plated fixtures SOLID
gold...Forget the Corbis Mona Lisa on those video
screens—I want the real thing NOW! After my plan
alterations, we should be able to get the cost up to a
nice even $100 million. Now, that's more like it...

TUESDAY, JUNE 3

Another show, another keynote speech...This
time it's Bill does Comdex, in sunny Atlanta. It's
tough getting a new (and interesting) permutation of
NT, Microsoft's billion dollar R&D spend, Moore's
Law, and the stupidity of NCs. So, instead, I came up
with the radical Q&A concept. Not stupid, off-the-
subject questions from those dummies in the audience either. But Bill-friendly questions that I came up
with a few days ago and fed to one of Microsoft's
tame journos. Ha! Sometimes they do have their
uses! (Sometimes I'm so smart it hurts. Yeaaaahhhh!)

Of course, the downside of shows is being away
from family and friends. (Well, family anyway.) But
modern technology makes it all easier. I'll be going
on plenty of cool, virtual cell phone movie dates with
Melinda and Baby Jennifer this week!

WEDNESDAY, JUNE 4

The next leg of the Bill Does America tour took me to Washington, home of Bill #2. This time I joined forces with Andy, Carol, Gordon, and other industry hotshots to lobby for, uh...software...you know, infrastructure stuff.

And this time it was Andy's turn to give a speech. He didn't mention Moore's Law even once. Well done, Andy! (These politicians wouldn't understand anyway. They're just not technical.)

THURSDAY, JUNE 5

Melinda says Ellison is a poor orphan boy, and that's why a big house is so important to him. No wonder he likes hanging out with Jobs...Two lonely orphan boys together—abandoned and unloved. Get over it, guys!

And don't forget, Larry...Second place is just the FIRST LOSER!

FRIDAY, JUNE 6

You have to give Carol Bartz credit. For an old chick—and a chick running a software company, too—she's not bad. While we were being driven around D.C. she came across as highly intelligent (for a chick) and well informed (for a chick). She certainly shares the Bill Vision Thing on software piracy. Autodesk is a big advocate of the death sentence for anyone caught with an unlicensed copy of AutoCAD. Hey, it's over $3,000 a pop—I'd be ticked off too. But that only addresses half the problem; you still don't get any money. Hmmm...How about death by lethal injection and a $300 fine (paid by the felon's estate) for anyone caught with MS Office—and no receipt! Sounds good to me!

SATURDAY, JUNE 7

Marengi (isn't this some kind of dance?) finally got canned by Novell: for bringing the company into disrepute by having a stupid name. I told you it was only a matter of time. In fact, poor Joe's being made a scapegoat for Novell's pitiful performance against the unstoppable NT.

Novell's a good example of the dilemma facing regulators—is it my ruthlessly competitive streak, or their natural incompetence? The two just kinda blur together, so that you can't tell where one ends and the other one starts. Which, I guess, is no bad thing.

Remember the Money deal? Where I convinced Frankenberg that Novell really wanted Money, while we were going to buy Quicken? I was SO good that day. Even the average man (or, as Melinda would say, person) in the street would have gone: "Right. You want ME to take this TURKEY off your hands, so that you can get regulatory approval for the Intuit deal, then kick our butts with Quicken. What exactly do we get out of it?" The answer was, of course, "What is absolutely nothing?" (I'll take Corporate Blindsiding for a thousand, Alex!)

You know, I really do try to get these WIN-WIN negotiations. Honest. I start the day off warm 'n' fuzzy, full of good intentions...But somehow, it all goes terribly wrong and we end up with the usual BIG WIN I GET EVERYTHING TOO BAD YOU JUST LOST YOUR SHIRT ON THIS DEAL SUCKER. I just can't help it, OK?

SUNDAY, JUNE 8

We have a winner! Barnes & Noble has another book about me! Cooooooooooool! This time it's *Overdrive* by James Wallace—with a way cool picture of me on the front. And what a writer! "As Chairman and CEO of Microsoft, the juggernaut of the software industry, he dominates the corporate landscape like a colossus." That's me, all right...

But hang on a moment. "The renowned visionary..." (right on, James!) "...missed the turnoff to the information superhighway..." This can't be true: I wrote all about the Internet in MY book. I knew about it all the time. (And anyone who says it was only in the revised edition is a liar.)

(Note: Wanna be cool? Wanna be irresistible to the opposite sex? Then buy a copy of *The Road Ahead* now!)

"Delete Philippe." MICROSOFT T-SHIRT

MONDAY, JUNE 9

Man! Don't you just love it when you sell a few of your shares and put nearly $300 million in your bank account? Now THAT'S what I call REALLY COOL.

Hmmmm...I think Nathan's hard at work on another article for *Slate*. I wonder what our other in-house visionary is writing about this time? He's OK...for a pudgy functionary whose most daring deed is to draft a boldly worded memo.

And more Diversity! We have a new Diversity Web site at Microsoft. Go, Randy! (Randy Massengale's our Diversity Manager.)

TUESDAY, JUNE 10

I saw Larry Ellison on *Late Night with Letterman*, or some other cheesy chat show, talking about his "vision." He looked good. I wonder if he paid for that camera angle.

What's Larry's vision? I think it's 20-15...but only with his contacts in. Still plenty good enough for spotting tall, twenty-two-year-old blondes. Who like rich, older men. Larry, you old dog! Mine, of course, is 20-20 with my cool specs. (So, as usual, I'm better than him. Nah, nah, nah-nah-nah...) And, I think I can show him a thing or two about scoring big with gorgeous young chicks...Oops... Sorry, Melinda, I was just kidding, OK?

WEDNESDAY, JUNE 11

I just got this e-mail message. I tell you: everybody loves me!

> Dear friend Bill!
> You just know that you are a big star and even bigger in San Jose! Do you know that all those 1,200 people who came to see you in ballroom Feirmont hotel were thinking: "He is the boss, he is cool, rich, smart, intelligent, young. Why not me?" Ha, ha, ha, ha. Did they really listened what you were saying. No way! They just kept thinking how to get you. But no way!!! You are not for a take!!! Right? This is so funny, do not you think? And keep going Mr. Bill Gates, God bless you and your family!
> Your friend—Elwira

Yeah, right on, Elwira! Especially that part about everyone thinking I'm cool, rich, smart, intelligent, young...I mean it IS true. And I really like your creative use of the English language, Elwira. Keep up that diversity!

THURSDAY, JUNE 12

You know that I'm not a vindictive guy...(Ambitious, competitive, ruthless, unrelenting, maybe, but definitely not vindictive.) So I think my "Stick It to Philippe" campaign should now be considered officially over...He thought he could compete with me, he thought he was more technical than me. Ha! I showed him!

I've crushed his little Borland company...(so now he ekes out a living with teeny-weeny Starfish Software)...I even "dated" his wife, Martine, back in her newly Philippe-less days! (She said mine was way bigger than his. And I don't think she was talking bank accounts. Hee, hee, hee.) And now I've stolen his friend and lead developer Anders Hejlsberg ...Revenge is sweet.

FRIDAY, JUNE 13

Our key mission has always revolved around the personal computer and how to make it more empowering and easier to use. One of the most important ways Microsoft continues to pursue this goal—and move the Windows buying revolution forward—is through its unique "customer feedback loop." (Honest...it's unique. No other company uses a customer feedback loop! I invented that too! I am just SO darn smart...)

At its most basic level, the customer feedback loop is how Microsoft keeps in touch with its customers and their needs. A multifaceted system, it enables Microsoft to collect vast amounts of information from customers—including their hardware, software, experiences, attitudes, suggestions, and bank balances—and utilize this data to continually create better products. And sell more stuff! (Big Brother is watching...)

SATURDAY, JUNE 14

FLAG DAY

Decided to compile my Top Ten Favorite Phrases:

1. Cooooool!

2. Way coooool!

3. Yeaaaahhhhh!

4. Rock 'n' roll! (Thanks Paul!)

5. High-bandwidth!

6. Into orbit!

7. Pre-preemptive.

8. Totally out of control bitchin' beyond belief. (Bitchin' for short.)

9. Boy, I'm a smart guy!

10. What a blast!

SUNDAY, JUNE 15

FATHER'S DAY

I had to stay in and pluck out those unwanted facial hairs. Man! You start hitting your forties and that facial hair grows faster than Microsoft stock appreciates. (OK, maybe not quite THAT fast.) Those nose hairs! That ear fluff! Those stray eyebrows! It's a jungle! It's a dirty job, but someone has to do it if I'm going to keep that clean-cut, high school freshman look that Melinda loves so much. You know, I'm not just rich...I still look about twenty-five years old. I have it all!

Helped Jennifer make a Father's Day card for superpop (that's me!) using Microsoft Greetings. What a great product! What a great company! What a great daughter! (My great genes, of course!) Into orbit!

"If you can dream it, you can do it."

ADOBE

MONDAY, JUNE 16

More praise for ME! Cool! Yet another chick on the Net who digs me...

To: Bill G.

From: Krista J.

Rich, funny, cute, and super-intelligent...Exactly as I pictured the Bill-man. Keep up the great work! Microsoft rocks!

Krista J.

So I said...

Thanks for the praise, Krista. You know I deserve it.

Regards, Bill G.

P.S.: Are you a babe? Scan me a pic, quick!!!

Hey, there's no harm in asking, right?

Yeaaaaaaaahhhhhhhhhhhhh!!!!!!

Jackpot! Just got a GIF (interlaced) e-mail attachment of young Krista...She is a TOTAL BABE! I am in nerd heaven...

To: Bill G.

From: Krista J.

Remember Cindy Crawford? Smarter, hotter, and richer.

If you morphed all five Spice Girls together, you'd get me. And I can zig-a-zig-ahh with the best of them!

XX00 Krista J.

P.S.: I love talking about the Internet, too.

WEDNESDAY, JUNE 18

Another week, another keynote. This time it was the Windows World conference in Seoul, Korea, where I was bringing enlightenment to a whole new bunch of slanty-eyed foreigners. (I didn't say that to THEM of course. Duh!)

Amazing! Korea is the seventh-largest PC market in the world. Do you know how many copies of Windows that is??!!

Steve Ballmer, my little bald Bill clone, stood in for me in New York at a PC Expo. "NCs are...Not Compatible!" he said. I've got him so well trained, he even uses my jokes. Cool!

THURSDAY, JUNE 19

Wow! Microsoft Japan has over 1,000 employees! That's our largest international subsidiary. And I get to tell everyone about my vision thing at the Windows TCO Summit. The Japanese love PCs, love Windows—and love me! That's Eastern Wisdom!

Tomorrow I'm speaking to a bunch of suits in Nagoya. Got my speech all planned—I'm going for short and sweet: *"Minna-sama, dozo yoroshiku one-gaishimas. Mo, Windows o katte kudasai!"* That's Japanese for, "Greetings honorable businessmen. Buy more Windows!" With language skills like that, nobody's going to call ME a gaijin! Is there no end to my talents? (Note: another trick question! Of course there's no end to my talents!)

You have to hand it to Paul Allen...he's no longer the soft touch that he was at Microsoft when he let me "slightly modify" our partnership agreement down from 50-50 to 70-30. I guess losing nearly $10 billion has made him a tougher negotiator. (What a fabulous ROI for a few hours arguing! I'm so smart!) So now he's insisting that Seattle coughs up $300 million to build a new stadium for his sports team, the Seattle Seahawks. Well done, Paul! (When you're down to your last few billion dollars, you gotta start watching those pennies!)

On the other hand, if Seattle agrees, this could be real bad...Paul will have TWO teams...and I'll still have none. No way!

Today, aspiring MBAs took their GMATs in test centers around the world. I'd been thinking of taking it, just to show Melinda that she's not the only one in the family who can get an MBA. But it's too risky. If I didn't score in the mid-700s my street cred would be blown forever.

Besides, with all those universities lining up to give me honorary degrees, why should I do actual work?

Went to Barnes & Noble. Bought *Men Are from Mars, Women Are from Venus.*

Melinda and I decided to have an early night. Melinda has her cooool IBM ThinkPad in bed, finishing the new PageWizard specification for Publisher 98. It's gonna be so cooool! I'm having a real blast reading the organic version of *The Catcher in the Rye,* one of my all-time favorite books. Guess I still feel like a smart kid just trying to figure the world out...

"There is no reason for any individual to have a computer in their home." KEN OLSON, DEC

Ha-ha! I just love it when Netscape screws up again and again! (Especially as it takes that spotlight off IE!) They've had big problems after some Scandinavian dude rejected the Netscape bug finder's fee claiming that his particular "major bug" was worth more than $1,000. To make matters worse, he claims that he called Netscape to report it and nobody was home! A big "Good work, Dude" to Christian O.! (And those rumors that I'm personally paying Christian to find Netscape bugs are just TOTALLY un-founded. Honest.)

Wow! Just imagine how much poorer I'd be if I paid out $1,000 to everyone who reported a bug (or, as we call it in our PR department, "inappropriate insect behavior") in a Microsoft product! Call me an old cynic, but there's something heart warming about the phrase "extensive public beta-testing." (Which, incidentally, I invented. I am just so smart!)

It's been said by some people that my obses-sion with the Spice Girls is a sign of immaturity and a lack of wider cultural awareness. Of course that's not true. EVERYONE knows that I am a well-rounded personality with an encyclopedic knowledge of many diverse areas. Life's NOT only about competitor crushing (although that's pretty cool). And to prove it (again showing Melinda my sensitive side), here's my Top Ten Classical Tunes:

1. Handel's Water Music

2. "Ode to Joy," from Beethoven's Symphony #9 (the Choral)

3. Rachmaninov's Piano Concerto #2 in C minor

4. "I Know That My Redeemer Liveth" (from Handel's *Messiah*)

5. "Jesu, Joy of Man's Desiring" (from Bach's Cantata #147)

6. "Adagio," from Elgar's Cello Concerto

7. *Finlandia*, Sibelius

8. "Ave Maria," Schubert

9. "Mon Coeur S'Ouvre à Ta Voix" (from Saint-Saëns's *Samson et Dalila*)

10. "Wannabe" (from *Spice*, by the Spice Girls)

THURSDAY, JUNE 26

So, I've been trying to get through to Larry E....I want him to come up to Microsoft Campus and tell us about his vision for the future. Then we can steal all his good ideas. Hee, hee, hee...But he just won't take my calls or answer my e-mail. Last chance, Larry, or I cross you off my Christmas card list...

Hey, Larry dude!!!!!!
I've been e-mailing you LOADS. But no reply so far. So...

1. Not getting the messages? (Due to crappy Oracle e-mail delivery systems?)

2. Both hands damaged by being trapped in a slamming door by an irate father of young Stanford co-ed, and hence totally unable to type any replies? (No voice recognition on your NC yet, huh?)

3. Unbelievably busy due to relentless self-promotion and hot new babe to keep satisfied? (Way cool!)

4. Just can't be bothered. (I thought so, you idle f***.)

5. Dead. (Oops. Don't I feel like the jerk.)

Delete as appropriate.

FRIDAY, JUNE 27

Hmmmm... What do I want to write about today? Java...thin client...Moore's Law...PC Success Loop...Internet...Zero Administration for Windows...scalability...Wallet PC...Wireless infrastructure...plug and play...Device ID...On Now... WebTV...symmetric multiprocessing...This stuff is just SO exciting! I love it!

Hey! What about...SQL...C++...ROM... DVD...SIPC...NT...PC...NC...RAM...WinCE... ISP...IBM (how did that one get in here?)... HTML...HTTP...Java VM...J++...SMTP... WDM...USB...IEEE1394...FTC...IRQ...CD... CPU...ISV...All totally fascinating stuff—beats me why people think the computer industry is dominated by obscure terms and acronyms. It's just so obvious to me...

SATURDAY, JUNE 28

Hey, Larry, old buddy! I've been thinking about your insatiable appetite for young chicks... Here's my Top Ten List of Larry's Ex-Girlfriends...

1. **Melissa**—the cute waitress down at the Yacht Club (nineteen)

2. **Jenna**—the Stanford business major (twenty-one)

3. **Charlotte**—the Swedish masseuse at that club in San Diego (twenty-three)

4. **Caroline**—a recent Miss USA (twenty-five, but too dumb!)

5. **Andrea**—the San Jose glamour model (twenty-seven, but WAY too dumb!)

6. **Tammi**—a software distributor's sales chick (thirty-two, and over the hill!)

7. **Kate**—one of the temps at Oracle (twenty-six)

8. **Melanie**—the blond babe from that PC Expo party (twenty-two)

9. **Nancy**—youngest daughter of one of the Oracle VPs (seventeen, yikes!)

10. **Adelyn**—another secretary at Oracle (twenty-nine, and she's still not getting that NSX)

I guess that takes care of the last three months or so, eh?

SUNDAY, JUNE 29

Big day on the caring, sharing husband front! Me and sexy M did that little billionaire-couple-stay-at-home-and-watch-a-video thing…Finally got to see the Batfilm…And I've decided to remodel the new pad: I'm replacing one of the garages with a secret passage leading to the Nerdcave where I'll keep my Nerdmobile!

Followed by a quick Chinese take-out…Her fortune cookie said, "You have a deep appreciation of the arts and music." Mine said, "You will be unusually successful in business." Cool! I guess that means I'm gonna be worth $50 billion, instead of a pathetic 35…

"Eventually, Microsoft will crumble because of complacency." STEVE JOBS

MONDAY, JUNE 30

Of course the Internet is all about standards, and allowing the wise American (and, I guess, those losers in the ROW) public decide what meets their needs. That's freedom of choice. That's the American Way. I'm all for it. And that means I'm 100% committed to having people make their own decision about whether to use IE or that other crummy browser whose name temporarily escapes me.

Today, I continued my fitness regime using my new invention: management push-ups. Did fifty! (Management—that's me—abuses his position of authority and forces a lowly code techno-weeny to do push-ups. Up, down, one...up, down, two...keep it up, three...concentrate on tighter, sharper code, four ...Phew! Pretty exhausting, I can tell you. But it proves my point: don't work harder, work SMARTER!)

TUESDAY, JULY 1

CANADA DAY (CANADA)

I've been talking with Melinda, and as a caring, sharing, '90s kind of guy, I've got a new mission ...I think "motherboard" is too gender specific, and I'm going to campaign to get it changed to "parent-board." And I know that Andy over at Intel is right with me on this one!

Surfing the Net to see if that UNOFFICIAL Bill Diary thing has been taken down...I can't wait to see an "Error 404—URL not found" message. Instead I find the "Bill Gates Wealth Clock." According to this site, on average, every man, woman, and child in the country has paid me $162. God bless America!

WEDNESDAY, JULY 2

It still seems to be mergers and acquisitions season...Electronic Arts (games dudes on the big downhill) have snapped up Maxis (the Sim-Stuff people), and the merger between Fractal and Meta-tools is now complete. Their blurb claims they've become the world's largest vendor of creative software... But that's us! So...they're more like the world's largest collection of brain-fried clueless acid heads!

The great thing about having a house with over twenty bathrooms is never having to ask, "Where do I want to go today?"

THURSDAY, JULY 3

Cool! Got back on the acquisition trail today and bought England's Cambridge University...it's a cute little European Harvard clone. Some of the biggest brains (other than mine) in the world are based there. Then I realized I'd gotten a little wild and bought the entire province, statelike, "county" thing of Cambridgeshire too! Apparently, it's called "Silicon Fen." What's a fen?

A research base in England is another stroke of (my) genius. Not only do they only have five channels, but it's one of the few countries that has an even worse climate than Seattle. These guys will have absolutely nothing to do except stay at the office 24/7 and invent supercool stuff...

FRIDAY, JULY 4

INDEPENDENCE DAY

God bless America! (And God bless Microsoft, too!)

Cool news! Part of the Cambridge deal was... Nathan's big buddy Stephen Hawking! He's mine! And Herman the German, inventor of the RISC processor! I hope Nathan's ego can cope...With Stephen on board, now there are two of us who are better at math and cosmology than him. (And one great new addition to the Microsoft Diversity program!)

SATURDAY, JULY 5

I don't believe it! That crummy Motorola company has announced plans for Celestri, a $13 billion global satellite network! They're stealing my

Teledesic idea! Everybody knows that I invented the satellite communications concept. Ha! You just can't trust anyone these days.

Luckily, I still have plan B...I just put $1 billion of pocket change into Comcast, the cable guys. As usual, I don't care which horse wins the race—I own all of 'em! (And even if I didn't, that's the great thing about being rich! I can afford to bet on every darn thing I think has a chance of winning.)

SUNDAY, JULY 6

Went to Barnes & Noble. Bought Paul Reiser's *Couplehood*. I'm going to master this relationship stuff if it kills me.

Apparently, VH1 is still playing the Rolling Stones video of "Start Me Up"...For twelve million bucks I thought I was getting EXCLUSIVE rights. (Lawyers at dawn! Maybe I can get a refund...It's not like I need the song anymore!)

Death comes to us all (unless, of course, my personal cryogenics project is wildly successful). Recent celebrity deaths include Jacques Cousteau (old French diver dude), Robert Mitchum (old actor guy), and James Stewart (another old actor guy). Each of them was surprisingly popular for a guy with no money and no computer inventions. I've got it! What a great idea for another Office Assistant! Harvey, the invisible, talking, superhelpful rabbit!

"Let's call the real world and try to sell something to it."

BILL GATES

Sometimes, when I'm sitting in my swanky office musing about the next competitor to crush...I find myself gazing out over our vast parking lot and watching the comings and goings of all my Microserfs in their Micromobiles...Here's my Top Ten Microsoft Bumper Stickers...

1. Try to make Windows idiot-proof and someone will make a better idiot.

2. Work is for people who don't have Microsoft stock.

3. Forget the Joneses, try keeping up with the Gateses. (This one's on Myhrvold's Humvee. Good luck, Nathan!)

4. Welcome to Dilbertville.

5. It's lonely at the top, but you eat better. (That's on my Lexus.)

6. The more people I meet, the more I like my PC.

7. All men are idiots, and I married their King. (This one's on Melinda's car. What can she mean?)

8. He who laughs last at Bill's jokes gets no stock options.

9. I get enough exercise just pushing my mouse.

10. According to my calculations, the problem doesn't exist. (Very popular with the IE development group.)

TUESDAY, JULY 8

I overheard a weird conversation between two project managers on Windows 98 today. One guy said "…I guess I was worried about signing the part that said I wouldn't work for a Microsoft competitor for five years if I leave…" His buddy replied, "That's no problem, you're not even doing any work here are you?" What could they have meant?

Hit the Internet Gaming Zone again. Man, we are SO cool! I kicked DingBat's butt at blitz chess! I told you I could have taken Deep Blue!

WEDNESDAY, JULY 9

In a major blow to Netscape Communications, Intuit announced that it will build my Internet Explorer browser into future versions of Intuit's market-leading (apart from Money, of course) personal finance software. Nah, nah, nah-nah-nah...I think I'm really getting the hang of this ruthless competition thing.

Called my broker and made sure that I get some stock in the @Home Network IPO on Friday. You can't be too rich, too thin, or have too many cable infrastructure investments.

THURSDAY, JULY 10

Big news over at Apple...CEO Gilbert Amelio (and his sidekick Ellen Hancock) has "resigned." Hee, hee, hee. Bye-bye Gil baby! Apple continues to go downhill faster than, uh...well, a really, really, fast going downhill thing. Put it this way: Apple's giving me the kind of industry competition that I know and love. (That's none! Perhaps I should have encouraged them to keep Gil on?) I told you right from the start that Gilbert was a loser. Boy, that $13 million in salary and bonuses—for less than eighteen months of one of the worst CEOs in computer history—sure looks like a sound investment, huh?

I guess this means that Steve will have a larger role as a "strategic adviser." That should fix their problems! Right. Hey! I know! Get him to renegotiate the contracts with those Apple cloners. (If I remember correctly, at the Apple worldwide developers' conference earlier this year, Jobs—tactful as ever—referred to the clone makers as "leeches.")

FRIDAY, JULY 11

MSN had 1.6 million members in

December. Now it has 2.3 million members. That's significant growth. Nearly 50%, in fact. I'm very satisfied. Oh yes, it's a complete success, which proves that my "Internet for Everyone" strategy is right on target. Exactly as I planned when we launched it: my business plan said we were going to be the #3 on-line service behind CompuServe and AOL. So...success as usual. I'm very happy. Really I am. Well done MSN team! Way to go!

SATURDAY, JULY 12

Far from being a chauvinist, I'm actu-

ally a big supporter of women in the industry. Honest. There's...

1. **Kim Polese,** Marimba (A definite BABE)

2. **Carol Bartz,** Autodesk

3. **Ellen Hancock,** Apple (Oops. Not anymore!)

4. Hmmmm...

5. **Martha Ingram,** Ingram Micro

6. **Melinda Gates,** Microsoft (Now, she's HOT!)

7. Uh...there aren't any more...

I noticed that Apple announced that the launch of Mac OS 8 will be on July 26. They obviously think this is going to turn things around. They must have some great Windows-beating features in store for us...Like... "Mac OS 8 is faster and more efficient than previous versions." Yeah? "Multitasking: you can empty the trash and copy multiple files at the same time." That's just SO cool! Oooh, I'm shaking in my boots! NOT!

Nathan and Stephen are going crazy about the Mars *Pathfinder* mission. Me? I'm finding it tough to get excited...Mars? No people, no PCs, no sales of Windows. So who cares?

"Only the paranoid survive."

ANDY GROVE

Great week for lists! I topped the *Forbes* Richest Dudes on the Planet list for the third straight year! Way cool! I'm showing Sam Walton (I thought he was dead?) and Warren Buffett and Larry Ellison (a pathetic #27!) how it should be done. Eat my dust, losers! Poor old Larry...How can you live on a paltry $7.1 billion?

$36 billion? Now THAT'S what I call a personal fortune. Here's that *Forbes* Top Ten:

1. **Me!** I'm just so cool!

2. **Waltons** of Wal-Mart (Isn't that the store for poor people?)

3. **Warren**, my buddy

4. Some **Hong Kong dude** I've never heard of

5. **Roche Pharmaceuticals** families in Switzerland

6. **Paul Allen!** (Microsoft stock rocks, huh?)

7. **Levi jeans family** (Nearly as good as Gap khakis.)

8. **More Hong Kong dudes**

9. **The Mars Bar people**

10. **BMW family**

TUESDAY, JULY 15

I'm just EVERYWHERE! I'm the richest, most powerful guy on the planet. I'm on CNN nearly every day! And after nearly seven years of headaches my neighbors can relax—my little waterfront techno-palace is just about ready for move-in!

And to think that just thirteen years ago, *Time* featured me and my "personal fortune estimated at

$100 million." Wow! Only $100 million? Those were the days! I may have been poor, but I was happy.

More great stuff in *Forbes*! How to make sure your prenuptial agreement is ironclad! Cool! After all, I wouldn't want Melinda walking away with $20 billion of my hard-earned retirement fund...

WEDNESDAY, JULY 16

Another e-mail from one of my fans!

To: Super-rich Bill G.
From: a Quark dude
Hey, Bill! But godDAMN you're RICH!!
What's the secret of your success? Tell me and I'll forward it to Tim Gill, the Pres, immediately!

Awesome! Maybe I can help my buddy Tim get rich too...He's done pretty well for someone who, basically, just has a slightly more expensive version of my go-getting Publisher product. Frames? He got that idea from me.

THURSDAY, JULY 17

I thought *Forbes* was, like, supercool. But they've blown their street cred with their totally random list of the Most Powerful Public Companies in the World. I don't believe it! Microsoft didn't even make the top ten!

And what's this International Business Machines outfit at #4? Is this a Fantasy League Company Top Fifty?

Hey, I forgot to include the bumper sticker on my old Mustang convertible in last week's list... "Honk if you think I'm sexy." I am, I am. The bigger the wallet, the sexier the man.

FRIDAY, JULY 18

Every day that I go to Microsoft is just one big buzz. I'll know that it's time to retire when I stop shouting "Wheeeee!" on the elevator at work! Then I'll hand it over to Steve "Slap-head" Ballmer. NOT!!!!!!!

Jeez. Wall Street. What do you have to do to keep these guys happy? Another great quarter...And the stock fell! GIVE ME A BREAK, LOSERS! Luckily, I'm still worth a cool $35 billion. Hee, hee, hee...

SATURDAY, JULY 19

Hey! This month's *PC Magazine* looks mighty fine...They've come up with the *PC Magazine* 100— the companies that make the personal computer what it is, and what it will be. We're Number One, we're Number One...Man, I love this magazine.

I don't like to criticize a former girlfriend, but Ann's numbers ain't that impressive...Her Hummer-

Winblad VC fund turned $30 million into $250 million. Sounds great until you realize that instead of risky start-ups she could have thrown it all into Microsoft…and made $3 billion. Now THAT'S what I call ROI!

Supercool! Kelloggs is running a free McDonald's meal coupon on selected boxes of Raisin Bran…Now I can enjoy my favorite cereal and save money on my favorite fast food. I'm such a thrifty guy! But, hey, you know what they say…"Look after the pennies, and the billions will look after themselves."

O.J. lost his mansion. Hmmmm…At $2.5 million it hardly qualifies as a mansion. A $50 million lakeside techno-palace—now THAT'S what I call a mansion.

"Content is where the real differentiated branded services will be offered."

BILL GATES

Man, I hate it when I have to do this…OK, Rob, you're not the total loser I thought you were when you said you were leaving us to develop an Internet sound thing. But I can't believe we couldn't do this stuff in-house! I suppose Nathan was too busy playing with his Humvee and writing *Slate* articles to develop some cool audio and video technology for the Net.

Instead I've had to eat a big slice of that humble pie and license RealAudio and RealVideo streaming technologies from Rob Glaser's Progressive Networks. And I'm sure we'll have to pay him way more money than he was getting when he worked here. That really hurts. I guess it wouldn't be so bad, but Rob really thinks that my management style sucks. That's so random! Would I be so rich if I wasn't a great manager?

It's almost worth buying the company just so I can get him back here and shout at him again. And, hey, it's definitely worth it to stop Netscape getting their hands on all that groovy Internet functionality. . . that will make IE so much better than Netscape's browser thing. (Whatever it's called these days.)

In fact, with the right spin it'll look like I planned it all along. Heck, I DID plan it all along. I knew Rob needed to follow his entrepreneurial instincts, and I encouraged him to make it on his own! He just needed that push to get started and develop this awesome technology.

And then I'll buy it. (Yeah! I'm just so smart!)

Hey! Check this out! I've just compiled a list of the Top Ten Richest (= Smartest) Guys in the Computing Biz. You'll notice that I have nearly as much money as the others COMBINED! That's how smart I am.

1. **Me!** (About $40 billion. What's a billion or so between friends?)

2. My buddy **Paul, Microsoft** (About $15 billion.)

3. My bald buddy **Steve, Microsoft** (About $9 billion.)

4. **Gordon Moore, Intel** (About $7 billion. Nice law, Gordon!)

5. My skirt-chasing buddy **Larry, Oracle** (About $6 billion. Loser!)

6. **Ted Waitt, Gateway** (About $2 billion. The only ponytail in the Top Ten.)

7. **Martha Ingram, Ingram Micro** (About $2 billion. Not bad for a chick!)

8. **Dave Duffield, PeopleSoft** (About $1 billion.)

9. **Michael Dell, Dell** (About $1 billion.)

10. **Charles Wang, Computer Associates** (About $1 billion. Not much, but he can console himself with his $6 million a year salary.)

In fact, if you laid the 500 wealthiest non-Microsoft executives from the entire computer industry end to end, the line would be over half a mile long. From the start of my new driveway, once around my house, across the landscaped grounds, and into the lake just past the end of my boat dock. But even together they'd still have less money than me! That's how smart I am.

But money isn't everything, and the novelty of being rich soon wears off—although the novelty of being the RICHEST lasts a bit longer. The other day, my net worth went over $40 billion and I really wanted to tell someone about my good fortune. But who? If I told Paul and Steve, they'd just complain that they don't have enough Microsoft stock. If I told any of my employees, they'd just ask for a raise. So I waited until I got home and told Melinda. She said, "That's great, Trey, but I have to take care of Jennifer right now. But don't forget, I get half." Man, what a downer!

In reality, great wealth isn't very exciting. I prefer sex. Yeaaaahhhhhhhh!

Big day at Microsoft as we did our annual schmooze-those-investment-analysts thing. It's simple...We dominate the software biz, and we're going to dominate the content biz. There's no end in sight for the growth of PC usage in developed nations, and growth in undeveloped nations is set to explode. Our revenues are just going to keep on getting bigger and bigger. We just can't help adding to that Microsoft cash mountain. And MSFT's going to keep going higher and higher. I'll soon be worth $100 billion. I'll be the richest man that's ever lived! Yeaaaahhhhhhh!

But we can't say that. So we told them the usual stuff about "strong competitors" (ha!), "cautiously optimistic" (sure!), "slower revenue growth," "earnings pressure," "sustainable stock price," and the rest. I think they bought it.

FRIDAY, JULY 25

But enough about me. What about those Apple guys, huh? They've announced the availability of supercool OS 8, the Mac operating system for the next...Millennium? Generation? Decade? More like the next coupla weeks.

It wasn't like this in the good old days when Jobs was running the company. Bring back Stevie! Oh, you've already tried that? And it's not working? Hee, hee, hee...

And yet another member of the board of directors (Delano Lewis) quit. That's four rats so far to have jumped from this particular sinking ship. Losers!

I think I was a little hasty in dismissing the Mars thing. After all, everybody else thinks Africa is a waste of time, but I'm investing in a new Microsoft subsidiary to exploit the future growth in one of the world's largest undeveloped markets.

I'm always looking ahead for longer-term strategic opportunities. So why not Mars? Microsoft Mars has a nice ring to it, don't you think? And the Microsoft...er, Mars government's Justice Department would, I guess, be totally supportive of our anticipated 100% market share for Windows, Office, and Money (Mars Edition). Restrictive OEM contracts? Great idea. Competitor crushing? What competitors? Death sentence for software piracy? Totally cool.

Where the heck is IE4? I know that Preview #2 is pretty cool, but don't you guys know that it's no good until it actually starts shipping to real customers and making us real money? (Or, at least, stopping Netscape from making any.) Luckily, we're right on schedule for that "end of Q4" release date that I promised.

No new books about me at Barnes & Noble...So I consoled myself by taking Melinda to see *Air Force One* on its opening weekend. I think Harrison Ford looks a lot like me. Obviously, he's not as buff, but that's good...the movie's otherwise totally plausible plot would be completely undermined if the president was too good looking.

"The information highway will break the tyranny of geography." NATHAN MYHRVOLD

MONDAY, JULY 28

Maybe it's my imagination, but everybody seems relaxed and enthusiastic today. Looks like my caring, sharing annual-company-picnic-event type thing over the weekend has reinvigorated my tired troops. Plus, I took the opportunity to give each of my VPs and senior managers a copy of *Zapp! The Lightning of Empowerment* by William Byham. Now that's what I call enlightened management: I can feel the positivity spreading through the office already! What does Rob Glaser know? I'm a great manager! I don't Sapp, I Zapp! I AM the lightning of empowerment!

TUESDAY, JULY 29

Does he, doesn't he? Will he, won't he? That's the gossip over at Apple this week, as they try to figure out where Steve "Visionary" Jobs fits into the picture. CEO? Chairman? Adviser? Like I could care less. But it's interesting that Stevie's playing so hard to get. It wasn't like this when John Sculley kicked HIM out all those years ago...If I remember correctly, he had to be dragged out of the building bawling his eyes out like a baby. It was so sad. NOT!

WEDNESDAY, JULY 30

On the investment front, Visa restructured
its e-commerce joint venture with Yahoo. In return for Visa's $300,000 investment over the last fifteen months, Yahoo gave Visa $21 million in stock to buy them out. A fine example of Bill-style deal making by Visa!

I'm so good with money: it doesn't matter where I invest Microsoft's huge cash mountain, it just keeps getting bigger. I couldn't get tax write-offs even if I tried. People think I'm so on the ball that even an investment in the Oil to the Arabs Corp. would automatically double in value as all those suckers pile in behind me!

Mergers and acquisitions continue...This week National Semiconductor snaps up Cyrix, so they can produce lots of those cheap NC things. Don't worry, Andy! Andy makes his own move by acquiring Chips & Technologies. This industry is just so much fun...

THURSDAY, JULY 31

I was thinking about creating a new push channel for *Slate* (I have to do all the work for that Kinsley guy!) using supercool IE4, but that Channel Definition Format (CDF) looks kinda complicated. It's at times like this that I'm glad I have 3,000 real programmers just waiting to execute that Bill vision thing...

Browser Wars? I don't think so. Battle of the Browsers? It's just not me. Nuking of Netscape. That's more like it, thanks very much.

FRIDAY, AUGUST 1

Japanese chick twins Kin and Gin celebrated their 105th birthday today. Man, these are the most wrinkled little people on the planet. But, for some reason, they're popular TV pinups in Japan. They must have even fewer channels than England...

Sooooooo...Stevie's not joining up, but my fifth-favorite billionaire (after me, Warren, Paul, and Steve) is. Good old Larry, still trying to turn Apple into an NC company, is going to be on the Apple board of directors and invest some of his millions. This saga could go on and on...

SATURDAY, AUGUST 2

Great new survey by consumer group Net-Action...Apparently, only three of the twelve major U.S. Internet access providers provide Netscape's whatever-it's-called-today as the default browser. That means the other nine feature my fabulous IE as part of their start-up kits...Well done, guys!

Saturday night is hot date night. Me and Melinda necking in the back row of *Men in Black*. Cool!

William Burroughs died today. No computer products, but famous for writing the seriously weird *Naked Lunch*. Which reminds me...I'll have to stop playing that game where I try to shoot a glass perched on Melinda's head. There's no telling what might happen...

SUNDAY, AUGUST 3

Isn't it ironic?

"Blessed are the poor...

Blessed are the meek...

Blessed are the merciful..."

Thirty years ago I learned the Sermon on the Mount. And today, I'm not poor, or meek, or merciful...Is there a moral to this story?

"Bill, thank you. The world's a better place."

STEVE JOBS (TAKING MY $150 MILLION)

MONDAY, AUGUST 4

ONTARIO CIVIC HOLIDAY (CANADA)

Just in case me and Rob Glaser don't see eye to eye (or he wants too much money for Progressive Networks) we've acquired VXtreme Inc.—a Silicon Valley developer of technology for sending audio and video over the Internet—for about $75 million.

This supercool technology will get integrated into NetShow and Site Server products and should boost acceptance of our hip and happening Active Streaming Format. Another Microsoft "Open" Standard. Cool! And just in time to head off support for Oracle's Video Encoding Standard API. You lose again, Larry! I'm just so smart!

TUESDAY, AUGUST 5

Supercool! Apparently, according to Nathan, scientists have just decoded the first message from an alien civilization. It says:

SIMPLY SEND 6 TIMES 10 TO THE 50 ATOMS OF HYDROGEN TO THE STAR SYSTEM AT THE TOP OF THE LIST, CROSS OFF THAT STAR SYS-

TEM, THEN PUT YOUR STAR SYSTEM AT THE BOTTOM OF THE LIST. NOW SEND THE LIST TO 100 OTHER STAR SYSTEMS. WITHIN ONE-TENTH GALACTIC ROTATION YOU WILL RECEIVE ENOUGH HYDROGEN TO POWER YOUR CIVILIZATION UNTIL ENTROPY REACHES ITS MAXIMUM! TRY IT. IT REALLY WORKS!

WEDNESDAY, AUGUST 6

According to press reports, Apple is on the lookout for a top-notch, customer-focused marketeer with vision and charisma who can rally the Mac faithful and attract new users. Vision and charisma...Hmmm...Now who does that remind you of? But, hey, I've already got a pretty cool job. I even get free soda. Sorry guys: you'll just have to make do with Stevie boy...

Who, I have to admit, was pretty good at MacWorld today...He announced a groovy new Apple board of directors and the cozy new Microsoft-Apple alliance. Me and Stevie are going to be big buddies from now on...I give him $150 million and he gives me the Mac browser market. (Suck on that, Andreessen!) And keeping Apple alive (albeit barely) keeps the FTC off my back. Hey, they still have 5% so it can't be a monopoly, OK?

THURSDAY, AUGUST 7

Cool! PBS suddenly finds that *Triumph of the Nerds* is supertopical and worth a rerun. Hot damn! I'm such a good looking guy—way better than Larry and Steve and all those other losers! I particularly like the bit where Steve talks about Microsoft's "third-rate products." Luckily for you our money's first-rate! It certainly saved your ass!

FRIDAY, AUGUST 8

That Apple stock has practically doubled already! $150 million for the Mac browser market? Peanuts! Now I'm making money on the stock too!

Plus, my Internet strategy really seems to be coming together pretty nicely, too. You know, it really does look like I had it planned all along...Sometimes I'm so smart, it hurts...

SATURDAY, AUGUST 9

No new books about me at Barnes & Noble. Instead I bought one of those great Tamagotchi egg things for Jennifer from Toys "R" Us. She loves it! I think I should do the Windows version...

At Microsoft Network they really know how to kiss my ass. But good...

Dear Bill,
Because we're your employees, we think you're
way cool . . .

Sincerely, MSN

SUNDAY, AUGUST 10

So I said:

Hi, MSN dudes:
Thanks for the support. I'll remember your kind
words at pay review time.

Sincerely, Bill G.

Do I mean it? Like hell I do. They have their
Microsoft stock options, so salary is irrelevant.

"Good artists copy, great artists steal."

PABLO PICASSO (& STEVE JOBS)

MONDAY, AUGUST 11

VICTORY DAY (RHODE ISLAND)

You know, I want to help, I really do. But does
Steve really deserve all this attention? It makes sense
for me to preserve this bunch of losers, but does it
make sense for the world's press to devote pages and
pages to a company with only 5% of the market?
Hold on, these figures just in...Down to 2.7%. Oops.

At least Stevie went straight to work on all the important stuff…aggressive new marketing campaign, boost sales, improved hardware margins, fab new technology, and getting that nextgen OS ready. NOT! Er…No cash bonuses, no business class flights, and NO MORE FREE SODA. I bet things are better already.

TUESDAY, AUGUST 12

One thing I have to say for Stevie is that he definitely puts his money where his mouth is. He's still holding ONE Apple share, so he really is fully vested in this turnaround situation. I mean, if he loses that last $30 he could be in deep doo-doo.

Apparently, Corbis DOES have electronic rights to Ansel Adams! But I'm so disappointed. I finally got some sample photos…and most of them are BLACK AND WHITE! It's just the same as those huge clip-art libraries with 100,000 images you see advertised—they just don't tell you that 85,000 are black and white highway signs and boring symbols. It just goes to show that you just can't trust anyone these days.

WEDNESDAY, AUGUST 13

Hey, it gets worse! They're all of mountains and lakes and trees and dull stuff like that. I've gone through them all and there's nothing interesting… No Porsches, no cool dudes break dancing, and no bikinied supermodels stepping out of the surf, covered in sand. Whose stupid idea was this?

Looks like the kids out there are totally "tickled" by Tickle Me Elmo, the sensationally popular Sesame Street doll that amused the likes of Rosie O'Donnell and the *Today Show*'s Bryant Gumbel last Christmas. Since Tickle Me Elmo first hit store shelves, nearly four million units have been sold! To meet the growing demands of Ticklemania, a Tickle Me Friends collection has been introduced, including a Tickle Me Big Bird, Ernie, and Cookie Monster. Looks like Barney the Dinosaur is KO'd. Er, how about a joint venture with Tyco?

THURSDAY, AUGUST 14

Now I'm cozying up to Marimba to work on more Microsoft Open Standards. So, maybe Castanet is cool… Or maybe this Java stuff might be interesting after all… Or perhaps this gets me closer to Kim baby—the HOT tech-CEO chick. She DEFINITELY wants to talk about the Internet. Yeaaahhhhhh!

All these joint ventures, strategic investments, and collaborative open standards might give people the wrong idea. I'm not admitting we can't do this stuff on our own. Of course we can. It's just easier if we can copy YOUR stuff first, OK?

ADMISSION DAY (HAWAII)

Microsoft wants the world to wake up to the joys of sex! It's official! Our research shows modern lifestyles mean that people spend too much time sleeping and not enough time enjoying marital relations. So now when you type "zzzz" into new Microsoft Word, it corrects it to "sex"! (And, in another big win for subliminal messages, if you type "software" it corrects it to "buy more Microsoft software.") Rock 'n' roll!

Which reminds me...Here are my Top Ten Dates with Melinda:

1. Night in with Ben & Jerry's from Costco, plus pretzels and Tab Clear...then rent a movie chosen using Cinemania.

2. A major Microsoft product launch (like Windows 98), especially the karaoke part...

3. Microsoft annual picnic.

4. Comdex keynote speech party.

5. Working late in the office, Melinda coming over with Ben & Jerry's, pretzels, and Tab Clear.

6. Virtual cell-phone-go-see-movie-in-different-towns date thing.

7. Real go-see-a-movie date.

8. One of those ball game things.

9. Shopping trip to the Gap to buy new outfits.

10. Shopping trip to Gap Kids!

SATURDAY, AUGUST 16

Today is the twentieth anniversary of the death of Elvis, the King. (One minute of silence here at Palace Gates.) And, for once, I won't criticize a dead rock star for his lack of computer inventions. In fact, Elvis is resonant with moral lessons for all of us. He shows me why I should not become a victim to my own money and fame, that I must resist the descent into decadence inspired by unheard of wealth and un-rivaled power. (And, for you poor people out there, he shows you that if you eat cheeseburgers while sitting on the can, it WILL end badly.)

SUNDAY, AUGUST 17

Big pop chick birthday weekend...Belinda Carlisle (ex Go-Go, today) and Madonna (yesterday) both hit the big thirty-nine. How about a cozy three-some talking about Java? Yeah.

Big day out at Barnes & Noble. Which shows you that the electronic experience (à la Amazon.com) just can't compete with actually HOLDING a book or magazine—and seeing my face on the cover. Way cool! And this week was a great one for me and my new Apple buddies...I make *Newsweek* (that's the most prestigious one), Stevie makes *Time* (he is not a good looking guy, is he), and Larry brings up the rear with *The Red Herring* (some kind of obscure fishing magazine, I think, discussing his Koi). $150 million couldn't even BUY publicity like this! Into orbit!

Actually, I think Larry confesses that he wants to be #1. Fat chance, dude. (Sometimes I wonder if his elevator goes all the way to the top floor.)

"Happiness is a stock that doubles in a year." STEVE BALLMER

MONDAY, AUGUST 18

Bummer! Looks like I haven't doubled my money on our Apple investment. Apparently, we didn't get nice ordinary, easily tradable shares... instead we got some crappy "convertible preference" shares. 150 million of the damn things for a buck each—and we have to keep them for, like, EVER. I don't remember being told about this. This is way uncool.

I guess that's what happens when you send a boy—young Greg Maffei—to do a man's job...

TUESDAY, AUGUST 19

Actually, here's the e-mail that I sent young Greg when I first heard about his great deal...

To: Greg Maffei
You bought what? You spent my $150 million on what? Don't you listen? I said "Snapple"!

The Internet is changing the fundamentals of organizational dynamics, market demographics, and the overall conduct of global commerce. It might be useful to examine some of the new paradigms emerging to replace traditional ways of thinking about business, career, and the pursuit of leisure. But, hey, then I'd have less material for *The Road Ahead II*...

WEDNESDAY, AUGUST 20

I just hate all the anti-Microsoft stuff that continues to float around. Especially after we do our White Knight thing and rescue struggling Apple... Do we pollute the environment? Nope. Do we infringe on human rights? No, sir. Do we test products on animals? Certainly not! Do we incite racial hatred? Absolutely not. (Our Diversity program makes sure of that.) Do we torture people? Negative to that one. Do our employees get FREE soda? Yep!

So why does the world hate us? Surely, no one's just a tiny bit jealous, are they?

THURSDAY, AUGUST 21

You know what the world needs now? Yup, ANOTHER search engine. We're working on a super-cool Microsoft Web tool—code-named Yukon—that's gonna kill the likes of Yahoo!, Lycos, Excite, and Infoseek. Just wait till you see it—it's outta control bitchin' beyond belief. (That means it's really, really good.)

FRIDAY, AUGUST 22

Hot news for pigs! You're officially the world's fourth most intelligent creature, following me at number one, men at two, and chicks at three. Bad news for Apple stockholders (excluding me), dropping one place to five, dolphins and whales, falling four places to six, and chimps, a nonmover at seven. In the lower part of the chart there's Europeans except the French at eight, European royalty at nine, and the French bringing up the rear, something they're very familiar with. (Larry Ellison is bubbling under at #11.)

SATURDAY, AUGUST 23

Although if pigs are so smart, why don't we ever eat dolphin-lettuce-and-tomato sandwiches, or order a salad with chimp-bits sprinkled on top?

Went to Barnes & Noble. No new books about me. Who else can these guys write about? Steve Jobs?

So...What do you get when you cross Apple with Microsoft? Microsoft!

SUNDAY, AUGUST 24

WINDOWS 95 DAY

Wow! It's the anniversary of the Windows 95 launch! What a way cool, completely outta control bitchin' beyond belief product that was!

No. It can't be true! They really are writing about Steve Jobs...I save his company, but they all wanna write about HIM...I just saw the latest magazine with an in-depth interview with the Boy Wonder. Why is he a "visionary"? I'm a visionary too. Why don't they call me a "visionary"? I'm tired of being "ruthlessly competitive." This guy got lucky too. I mean, you know, they always say I got lucky when IBM licensed DOS. That wasn't luck, it was skill. I negotiated a great deal from IBM then ran over to Patterson's place and snapped up Q-DOS. That takes BALLS. Jobs has no balls. Jobs is a guy who spends two weeks choosing a washer/dryer. Yes, TWO weeks. For what? Like, $500 or so. The guy has millions. Jobs is a guy who actually cares about his clothes "feeling really soft." What a loser...

Melinda says Jobs is a poor orphan boy, and that's why family stuff is so important to him. But, she says, he DOES have a point about the clothes being soft...

(Insert silent scream here.) I want a divorce.

"Nothing in fine print is ever good news."

A MICROSOFT PARTNER

MONDAY, AUGUST 25

And here's my Top Ten Overhyped, Overmentioned, Makes-Me-Sick list for the week:

1. **Apple**

2. **Steve Jobs**

3. **Riven: the sequel to Myst**

4. **Riven: the sequel to Myst, beta version**

5. Those **Myst/Riven Miller brothers**

6. **Larry Ellison**

7. **Justice Department investigations**

8. **NCs** (Network Computers, stupid.)

9. **Marc Andreessen**

10. The phrase **"Marc Andreessen reminds me a lot of Bill Gates when he was twenty-five."**

Anyway, who wants Myst when you can have Microsoft Return of Arcade? One basic 3D fantasy/mystery thing against four towering pillars of mesmerizing gameplay glory. It's like choosing between *Men in Black* or a four-movie-mega-bill of *Star Wars, Return of the Jedi, Terminator 2,* and *Jurassic Park.* No choice at all for anyone in their right mind.

Jobs doesn't even have as much money as me. How can he be smart? And it's not like he's better looking than me. He's definitely a loser...

Got down and did ten (old-fashioned) push-ups. Anger is power.

WEDNESDAY, AUGUST 27

Sitting in my office today, busy saving the planet, when I get some e-mail from Melinda. It's her Top Ten Reasons That PCs are Male...

1. Size does matter.

2. They'll do anything you want if you press the right buttons.

3. Despite years of evolution they can't think for themselves.

4. It's easy to turn them on.

5. They never live up to the marketing claims.

6. Even the best ones are unreliable.

7. You always need a backup.

8. They look great until you get them home.

9. An improved model is always just around the corner.

10. They are full of data, but remain clueless.

I don't get it. Does postnatal depression last a year?

THURSDAY, AUGUST 28

Today I pondered a serious question that's been running through this industry of mine right since the start...beards. I've always made the decision to remain boyishly clean shaven (the high school freshman look), but it's a decision not made by many of my peers, competitors, and minions. Why do so many grow beards? Would they be more productive without beards? What about those goatee things? Does grooming reduce the amount of time you can devote to thinking (and competitor crushing)?

FRIDAY, AUGUST 29

I suspect that contact lenses are pretty time-consuming too. Solutions, eye exams, putting them in and out. Phew! I feel tired already. Glasses are way more efficient. I just slide these babies on and go. And it's not true...chicks do make passes at men in glasses...

> Hey Bill, you smart-looking sexy babe:
> Is it true that you have hair on your chest like Roger Moore? Are you just as sexy as you appear in your photos? Are your glasses heavy and are they built like the bottom of two Pepsi bottles?
>
> Yours faithfully,
> the two Swedish girls in Denmark

Yeeeeaaaaahhhh!

SATURDAY, AUGUST 30

Now that I think about it, this shower-every-morning thing that Melinda insists on seems way over the top, time-wise. I mean, like how much can a guy sweat writing VB? Yeah, and I'm pretty sure that one shirt can last for a week too, provided you hang it up at night to air.

SUNDAY, AUGUST 31

In fact, I got this e-mail on the personal grooming issue.

Bill Gates, you're my hero...
Could you possibly tell me where you get your hair cut? I've been really groovin' for a sh'nazzy do...and you've got the hip-hoppiest one around...I saw once when you were doing an interview, and I saw your makeup artist *actually* comb your hair...into what it looks like normally...I thought it was just naturally groovy like that...boy was I heartbroken to learn that if I wanted a kick-ass haircut like yours I'd have to be followed around by a Microserf too...

Catch ya later, big brother...Ben

So it's not just chicks who dig my personal style! I'm a role model! Yeaaahhhh!

Tragedy! Diana, Princess of Wales, was killed today in a horrific Paris car crash. I guess that's one more rich, hot chick that I'll have to cross off my prospect list. And I never did get to talk to her about the Internet.

"Success is a lousy teacher, and an unreliable guide to the future." BILL GATES

MONDAY, SEPTEMBER 1

LABOR DAY

Summer's almost gone, and I was just sitting here wondering how Dr. Schmidt was doing over at Novell...Who cares! I guess Novell just didn't notice the Internet—and the rest is history. It's a good job we were so way ahead of the game on that one! Maybe Netscape will buy Novell—that would finish Marc at one stroke!

And, unbelievably, the FTC is checking out our Apple investment. It's just not fair. I want justice for Microsoft. I'm the smartest, richest man in the world—and they're jealous!

Here's one that really makes my day...We're about to get some pocket change in damages from some teeny company for one of those "sold our PCs with DOS installed, but didn't know we had to send Bill a check" cases. Their defense goes along the lines of "We didn't know the copyright to DOS is owned by Microsoft." As if! Everyone knows who owns DOS. (And as long as nobody calls Ray Noorda as an expert witness, we should be fine.)

TUESDAY, SEPTEMBER 2

Spent my lunch break at Barnes & Noble. Still no new books about me. So, instead, I bought Feynman's *Lost Lecture,* a book about my favorite modern scientist, Richard Feynman. I'll never forget the time I spent with Ann Winblad watching a series of his great physics lectures. Like me, he was good looking, witty, and brilliant. And, like me, he enjoyed spending time with hot chicks (although, sadly, as a happily married man, those days are behind me). It's interesting to note that even Feynman was unable to follow the math in Newton's *Principia*, which I found pretty straightforward. I rock, math dudes!

WEDNESDAY, SEPTEMBER 3

Ah, Ann... Boy, the memories came flooding back. Ann was pretty influential (in my pre-Melinda days, of course). She also introduced me to biotechnology, and showed me how significant this stuff would be. In fact, if I wasn't at Microsoft, I think I'd be working in biotechnology. I expect to see breathtaking advances in medicine over the next two decades, and biotechnology researchers and companies will be at the center of that progress. The emerging medical revolution, spearheaded by the biotechnology industry, is critical to the future of humankind. The biggest breakthroughs in medicine will result from the mapping and understanding of the human genome—figuring out the exact sequence of the three billion nucleotides that make up the estimated 100,000 genes that are the collective blueprint for human beings.

Of course, the big attraction is the huge P/E ratios of these biotech companies. That means more money! Maybe my lucky investment streak will continue with ICOS and Darwin. Cool!

THURSDAY, SEPTEMBER 4

Actually, while not wanting to give Ann ALL the credit, she also got me to start Corbis, a company I founded in 1989 that is entirely separate from Microsoft (just in case the unthinkable and unimaginable happened). The mission of Corbis has been to take images of all types—from great photographers like Ansel Adams, from leading museums, and from historical collections such as the Bettmann Archive—and make them easily accessible in electronic form. We're digitizing images at very high quality, and we'll make it straightforward for people to use the images. (Well, we'll certainly make it easy for people to PAY to use the images! Hey! This stuff costs me money.)

Wow! Saw the Spice Girls LIVE on the MTV Music Awards. Cooooool! They dedicated both their performance and their award (best dance video for "Wannabe") to Princess Diana—the other Spice Girl.

FRIDAY, SEPTEMBER 5

I'm very excited about Corbis. I expect most of its transactions to take place on the Internet. Eventually millions of people all over the world will have access to electronic images from the Bettmann Archive, including the entire UPI (United Press International) photojournalism library. The idea that millions of people will be able to draw on millions of images would have been almost unimaginable only a few years ago. It's exciting to help play a role in making this happen. And, even at just a few cents an image, think of the revenue stream! And it's all mine! Yeaaahhhhh! Thanks Ann!

Another famous chick died today...This time it's Mother Teresa of Calcutta. Now back to the Princess Diana coverage...

Larry King got married today, for the seventh time. Or was it the eighth? Apparently he's lost count. Another triumph of optimism over experience...

SATURDAY, SEPTEMBER 6

Ann was really a smart chick. And rich too. And a lot of fun (if you know what I mean). I guess basically she was too short and too old, and I couldn't bring myself to give her the baby Bill that she craved. Life is hard sometimes. But, hey, I ended up with a younger, taller, and better-looking woman (by marrying my darling Melinda) and bouncing Baby Jennifer. So I'm OK. Life is good. Rock 'n' roll!

Steve Case keynote at the SPA Conference. Today he claimed ten million users. Another made-up-number alert!

SUNDAY, SEPTEMBER 7

And, naturally enough, I hear that the eighteenth hole on the Hawaiian golf course where I got married has become a kind of shrine! A variety of computer industry types (both lower order nerds and higher order executives) have been spotted rolling around on the green, "trying to pick up some of Bill's karma, man." I really am a role model. Yeaaahhhhh!

"If the wind blows hard enough, even turkeys can fly." PHILIPPE KAHN

MONDAY, SEPTEMBER 8

I love new Microsoft FrontPage 98—the easiest and fastest way to create and manage a Web site. And, boy, is it easy and fast? It sure is. If you can click, drag, and drop, you can do it! It really is the best tool for creating and managing professional Web sites without programming. This baby kicks NetObjects Fusion's butt. (Another crummy IBM investment!) Into orbit!

TUESDAY, SEPTEMBER 9

Although, I should have added that FrontPage 98 is available from a reseller near you (or from the Microsoft booth at Windows World, Dallas). Go buy it now…because I get $17.40 from every sale! Yeaaaahhhhh!

I'm still a role model...

Dear Bill:
Like you, I am a good-looking computer nerd and seem to have a problem meeting women. I was wondering, with your looks, brains, and charm is there a good opening line that I can use to start a conversation that may last longer than two minutes?

Tom L.

How about: "Gates. Microsoft. Bathroom. Now!" Oops. You can't use that one. (Well, not without me suing your butt off.) "Yo, babe, I'm the richest man in the world." Aaaargh! Nope! How about the honest approach? "Hi, I'm a computer nerd, but according to *Time* magazine, computer nerds are cool right now..."

WEDNESDAY, SEPTEMBER 10

Here's my Top Ten Ways a Cool Software Guy (Like Me) Can Impress His Date (Melinda, of course):

1. If you're getting serious, consider a set of "his 'n' her" system-unit keys.

2. Flash the big wads of tens and twenties you created with Microsoft Image Composer and your color laser printer.

3. Spend an evening playing floppy disks backward, listening for the secret messages about Satan.

4. Invite her back to your place to show her the etchings on your Newton MessagePad. (Worked for Jerry Kaplan!)

5. Let the lady go first when you reach the virtual-reality escalator.

6. Serenade her with Microsoft Music Producer and your MIDI-compatible drum pads.

7. Have your dinner illuminated by the soft glow of an active-matrix LCD panel.

8. Drive her crazy by murmuring tender love words with the help of a French-speaking voice synthesizer.

9. Never type on your date's laptop computer without permission, particularly if the system is on her lap.

10. When things get tough, simply ask yourself, "What would Larry Ellison do in a situation like this?"

THURSDAY, SEPTEMBER 11

How are my lawyers doing with that UNOFFICIAL Bill Gates Diary thing? I will stop at nothing to get that vicious imitation of my diary off the Internet.

Have the author killed. No, wait, pay him $5 million. My lawyers explained that either solution would violate freedom of the Web. OK, then have him killed. My lawyers noted that this would only confirm people's unfair preconceptions about Microsoft. Then offer him $10 million! Sadly, the author is no doubt far too principled to accept. NOT! Just have him killed...

FRIDAY, SEPTEMBER 12

Microsoft is the proud sponsor of today's Economic Empowerment Conference for Small, Minority, and Women-Owned Business. That's diversity!

I think the secret of my success is simple: I keep my feet on the ground, my head in the stars...and a big bowl of strawberry Jell-O under my pillow, just in case I get hungry in the middle of the night.

SATURDAY, SEPTEMBER 13

Melinda and I just watched *Independence Day* on video. Totally noncredible! AS IF! I mean, the alien mother ship's operating system wasn't even Windows!

SUNDAY, SEPTEMBER 14

I've been checking our Windows sales, and while they're good, they could always be better. So here's my Top Ten Reasons to Buy Windows 98...

1. The access number for AOL is always busy, so you'd rather join MSN. And there's an icon RIGHT there!

2. Fewer Mac sales will mean GOOD-BYE STEVIE. Yeeeaaaahhhh!

3. It's just the excuse you need to upgrade your system.

4. You want plug and play.

5. Your mom is a Mercedes dealer in Seattle.

6. The Internet is too full of information, so you'd like me to decide what you should see.

7. You think the Justice Department should be fighting monopolies not crime.

8. Microsoft Bob.

9. You always wanted Microsoft to maintain a database of your hard drive. That way you'll never miss out on an upgrade offer. (Ha, ha.)

10. Do you know how much it costs to build a 40,000-square-foot-house in Seattle?

"I'm still kind of pumped from using the mouse." DILBERT

MONDAY, SEPTEMBER 15

One of the guys in the office sent me an e-mail message: "Bill, what's it like to be the richest man in the world?" I thought about ignoring him, but, hey, it's a fair question. On the one hand, it brings enormous pressure and responsibility as I continually seek ways to move technology and mankind forward. On the other hand...it rules! What's it like to be a poor person? I've forgotten. Ha, ha.

I'm tired of all this Justice Department hassle. The things you see Microsoft doing, like innovative content, lower prices, and things like that, it's sort of what capitalism wants to happen. SO GET OFF MY CASE, OK!

TUESDAY, SEPTEMBER 16

A cool seventy million copies of Windows! Michael Jackson eat my dust! We've left *Thriller,* the best-selling album of all time, trailing in the dust! And I get over $10.00 (personally) for every copy sold! I bet he only gets a couple of bucks at the most. And I've never been accused of child molesting. And my nose is still entirely original.

WEDNESDAY, SEPTEMBER 17

I've decided that Gap polo shirts are passé. Even the neat pink ones. No, the hip thing now on campus is a Cutter & Buck—the world's best basic shirt—with Microsoft logo. 100% combed-cotton deluxe jersey, fine weave twill placket and neck taping, custom buttons, generous fit, stripped collar and sleeve rib. Now THAT'S what I call cool...

What gives with Madonna? First she stops wearing those cool fingerless lace gloves, and now I've just heard that she's sold that famous black satin bustier with the huge conical tips and tassels. What is the world coming to? You know you're getting old when your popular-music sex symbols are giving it up for motherhood and baggy dungarees...And only $15,000...If I'd known, I'd have bought it for Melinda (she has the fingerless gloves already). There's nothing I love better than Melinda doing "Like a Virgin" just before bedtime. Hee, hee, hee...

THURSDAY, SEPTEMBER 18

Melinda and I had a test today to see who's best at producing anagrams—a great test of mental agility. We picked "information superhighway" as the topical starting phrase and gave ourselves ten minutes...

Melinda came up with "Hey, ignoramus—win profit? Ha!" and "Waiting for any promise, huh?" and "New utopia? Horrifying sham!" and "Inspire humanity, who go far" and "A rough whimper of insanity" and "Oh, wormy infuriating phase." Well done, baby.

I came up with "Enormous hairy pig with fan." Hmmmm...

But I was multitasking how to crush Netscape, OK?

FRIDAY, SEPTEMBER 19

I've heard a rumor that one of the TV networks is thinking of producing a drama series loosely based on my life. They're trying to entice Matthew Perry and David Schwimmer from *Friends* to play me and Paul in our early days at Harvard, sharing an Altair...I'm not sure they're good looking enough to play me, but, hey, these networks think they know it all. Ha!

Bill #2 drops young Chelsea off at Stanford for that education thing. Another eleven years or so, and I'll be doing the same for Baby Jennifer. She's just like her pop: cute, precocious, and rich.

SATURDAY, SEPTEMBER 20

Oh-oh... Looks like competition on the giving-it-all-away-to-charity front. Ted Turner isn't content to use the (IMHO perfectly plausible) "I'll give it all away later" approach. He's pledged $1 billion over ten years (that's $100 million a year, I think) to the United Nations for international aid. Looks like I might have to review my strategic donations plan if I'm to maintain my position in the Charity Top Ten. Damn!

SUNDAY, SEPTEMBER 21

Today marks the staging of the first annual Microsoft Silicon Valley Marathon. With my backing, it's destined to become one of the most significant marathons on the international circuit. I would have entered, but...er, I have a twisted ankle. Maybe I should go down to Oracle Open World instead. I'm sure Larry would be good for a few laughs...

Went down to Barnes & Noble, but found no new books about me. However, I picked up a copy of *Time*...which has redeemed itself with the list of the Top 50 Cyber Elite. I'm Numero Uno! I'm just so cool. Although why I have to share the honors with Ballmer and Myhrvold is a bit of a mystery...Still, I guess we're grooming them for stardom so that I can retire and spend...er, I mean GIVE AWAY...all my money.

And I'm still ahead of Murdoch, Levin, Ellison, and Jobs. Yes!

"Wealth is the product of man's capacity to think." AYN RAND

MONDAY, SEPTEMBER 22

Am I good, or what? Microsoft Office automatically fixes typing errors and corrects spelling, remembers your appointments, and schedules your meetings. Microsoft IE4, on your Windows 98 Active Desktop, goes to the front of the line for you at the ticket office or the airlines, and snoops around the world for the title of that Pulitzer Prize–winning novel from 1963 that you can't remember. Microsoft Bookshelf helps you do your research and cross-referencing and looks up the word *sesquipedalian* and, in a nice friendly voice, tells you how to pronounce it. Microsoft Money balances your checkbook, double-checks your bank's sums, and runs all the figures to see if remortgaging (Note: I must ask Melinda what a mortgage is) is a good idea or not. Microsoft software will happily handle mindless chores. Unless, of course, you work at Netscape and like that sort of thing.

TUESDAY, SEPTEMBER 23

Dr. Pop back at the pop desk! Wrinkly old rockers the Rolling Stones kick off their Bridges to Babylon world tour, just in advance of releasing the new album. Supercool! I hope I'm still churning out the software hits when I'm in MY sixties...

With Apple now bundling Microsoft Office and Internet Explorer with Macs, it's just like the good old days! As the world's largest Mac software developer I feel that this confirms our enlightened thinking. We're so generous that even people using outdated, inferior, and obsolete hardware can have the pleasure of using Microsoft software. And it's great to lie awake at night and imagine how Stevic must have felt making that bundling decision down in Cupertino (and BEGGING me for the $150 mil)!

WEDNESDAY, SEPTEMBER 24

It's great being a media mogul! Since I got MSNBC and *Slate,* I'm never out of the news! And it's all positive, too! Hey, who says editorial control is a bad thing? It's done wonders for my popularity with a 97.3% increase in fan mail (by volume, after seasonal adjustments, based on the corresponding period of fan mail in the preceding quarter). And I now control over 90% of the technology CEO fan-mail market. Of course, I don't count autograph signings at public appearances in retail stores because that's a tiny, insignificant market that I have no interest in. (Steve Jobs is welcome to it.)

THURSDAY, SEPTEMBER 25

And I'm getting back on top (heh, heh, heh) of the "e-mailed sexual suggestions from female fans to technology CEOs" market. After a late start (I was busy building Microsoft), I now control nearly 40% of this emerging high-tech market...And while I haven't calculated an exact growth rate, last week I only had 3.6% share. Explosive growth—even by Microsoft standards!

FRIDAY, SEPTEMBER 26

Inspiration! E-mail marketing... "At Microsoft, quality is job 1.1."

SATURDAY, SEPTEMBER 27

Last night, at my local Shop 'n' Save with Melinda, my eye was caught by the "50% Extra Free" slogan on a large box of Raisin Bran. I mean, you have to watch the pennies. You can understand my disappointment this morning, when, instead of my usual toast, I decide to have some brand-new Raisin Bran...I pour some into my bowl, but it doesn't have any raisins. So I stop pouring (the bowl's about half full) and (guessing that the raisins have simply settled to the bottom) shake the box contents vigorously before filling my bowl. No luck. Still no raisins. So I pour the bowl contents back into the box, and holding the end of the inside bag closed, I turn the box upside down (the raisins are denser than the bran, right?) and, again, shake vigorously. I pour again. And still no luck. Finally, I take the plastic bag out of the box and shake it while watching it carefully to see where the raisins go. Where do they go? Nowhere, because there aren't any! My conclusion? There simply aren't ANY RAISINS in my RAISIN BRAN!

SUNDAY, SEPTEMBER 28

Now, it's not that I'm anal or anything, but that Raisin Bran really ticked me off. I don't know how technical those Kelloggs guys are, but here's the scoop: bran is boring. The only reason people eat bran is because they think it's healthy and good for them. No one actually likes bran. And that's why raisins are great: they're chewy, juicy, tasty, and fun. That's what turns tedious bran flakes into Raisin Bran, a hit cereal. I'm going to e-mail Mr. Kellogg, RIGHT NOW, and complain...

"I'm so much more limited by time than by money." BILL GATES

MONDAY, SEPTEMBER 29

This week it's the Seybold thing: another show, another Bill keynote speech. Boring. But these shows give the people a chance to come up and tell me how great I am. Freedom of expression really is a wonderful thing.

What a load of kiss-ass guys there are out there!

TUESDAY, SEPTEMBER 30

Windows 98 and NT 5.0 may be late, but

IE4 was released today, RIGHT ON SCHEDULE. I love it when we get it right. And I love taking Melinda to a big Microsoft launch party...Fort Mason in San Francisco was supercool! Everyone who was anyone—Steve Ballmer, Nathan Myhrvold, Paul Maritz—was there! And I got to talk about supercool IE4 and how EVERY ISP in the WHOLE WORLD has agreed to include it as their preferred browser.

And the absence of Kevin Bacon and the Spice Girls was barely noticed. I wasn't a bit disappointed. Oh no.

And Marc Andreessen wasn't there either. But HE didn't get an invite. Nah, nah-nah, nah-nah...

WEDNESDAY, OCTOBER 1

So Marc Andreessen thinks that Netscape has this huge competitive advantage by being based in Silicon Valley, does he? All cozy little partnerships and joint ventures, is it? Well Marc, that's not going to be much use when California slips into the ocean, is it? And, according to my research, there's a good chance you boys will be taking an extended swimming lesson in the next twenty-four months! Way cool!

Back at Microsoft Campus. Home Sweet Home. Even when it comes to kissing my ass, Microsoft guys are the best...

THURSDAY, OCTOBER 2

FIRST DAY OF ROSH HASHANAH

Had to interrupt an important Microsoft counting-the-downloads-for-IE4 meeting when my Tamagotchi started beeping for attention. Jennifer just hasn't grasped the concept of feeding, entertaining, and cleaning...So I've had to take over. The things I do for that girl...Boy, I just can't wait for the Windows version to come out...

Apparently, Marc Andreessen thinks he's the next Bill Gates...Ha! I could carve a better man out of a banana!

FRIDAY, OCTOBER 3

You know, I'd like to squash Jim Barksdale and Netscape just like a bug! Boy, it's going to be great wiping THAT off my shoe!

Yeaaahhhh! Best day this week. Kelloggs has responded to my e-mail and sent me a $3 money order (to cover my costs) AND a store coupon valid for $3 of Kelloggs products. Melinda! Let's get down to Shop 'n' Save right now!

SATURDAY, OCTOBER 4

Anniversary of the death of Seymour Cray, the father of supercomputing. Hey, none of his computers ran Windows (any version), so what do I care?

Rock 'n' roll! Over 1 million downloads of IE4! Into orbit! I couldn't resist a quick e-mail to Marc over at Netscape...

Marc:

As leaders of the software industry we should try to work together, even though, as competitors, there is sometimes discord. You've done a great job in establishing the Internet, but I'll be happy to carry on from here.

Regards, Bill G.

P.S.: IE4 rocks! Over 1 million downloads already! Into orbit!

Went to Barnes & Noble. Bought *Microserfs* by some dude called Douglas Coupland. I just don't get it. "The real significance of Microsoft lies in the infoserfs, not the cyberlord." Huh? Although "Bill, be my friend...please" sounds about right. Ha, ha!

Received a prompt reply from Marc at Netscape:

> Bill:
>
> Thank you for your comments. We at Netscape are committed to supporting Open Standards and providing greater freedom of choice to our customers.
>
> Marc A. (still only twenty-five)
>
> P.S.: Our site gets over 80 million hits a day, and we have 50 million Navigator users. Beat that!

"We must not forget the obvious: disks are round."

NICHOLAS NEGROPONTE

Actually "Open Standards" is quite funny. Netscape's home page locks out non-Navigator browsers. Netscape is the company that doesn't provide documented interfaces for Navigator and its plug-ins. We document EVERYTHING with IE. (Oh yes we do.) I wrote:

> Marc:
>
> I want to add JavaScript as a plug-in to Navigator, but you don't publish the interface specification. Please give it to us.
>
> Bill G.
>
> P.S.: Usability Sciences confirm that 89% of people prefer IE4 to Navigator. Yeaaaahhhhh!

TUESDAY, OCTOBER 7

CompuServe, AOL, MSN, Prodigy, MCI, AT&T WorldNet...What do these on-line services have in common? Yup, they all have my awesome IE as the "preferred browser" (that means default, dummy). Cool! Hey, Marc, what d'ya think of that? We'll be at 50% market share this time next year—mark my words!

In the end, market share in the browser market will be determined by technical excellence and marketing savvy. With IE4 we've already achieved technical superiority over Netscape Navigator. (Oh yes we have!) And our latest distribution deals mean that we're dominating the new user segment.

In fact, I was thinking that "forever" is a long time. I'd guess that free "for the next year or so" should be sufficient! (It's not as catchy though, so I don't think I'll e-mail marketing with THAT suggestion.)

WEDNESDAY, OCTOBER 8

It's good to be humble. I still keep an old CP/M machine running the GEM GUI, that old clunker developed by DR and used on the Atari ST. It looks pretty quick. I'm going to try a Commodore 64 and run GEOS on it! Maybe it would make a great $500 NC? Maybe I can do one of my famous joint ventures...McDonald's could sell them in Happy Meals as the MicroMcGeo64 NC.

THURSDAY, OCTOBER 9

On the other hand, why be humble? Lotus, Apple, WordPerfect, Borland, etc., did a good job of crushing themselves. They could all be dominating their markets if they were more competitive. I watched their downfall wondering why they were such a bunch of screwups. I thought their course of action should have been obvious. Microsoft was the only company that consistently went in the right direction and even told everyone in advance where they were going. I rock, dudes!

FRIDAY, OCTOBER 10

Corel has announced that CorelDRAW! 8 will ship real soon now. Right.

Marc (die, die, die) A., replies...

Bill:

Thank you for your comments. We at Netscape are committed to supporting Open Standards and providing greater freedom of choice to our customers. Even Microsoft.

Marc, xoxoxo

P.S.: Did you know that independent market research shows that Navigator has over 65% market share? Nice metric, huh, Bill?

SATURDAY, OCTOBER 11

YOM KIPPUR

Really, Marc, this market share research can be VERY misleading. I like to think of research into what people already have as "trailing edge" analysis. It tends to promote the status quo. Of course, for mature markets, such as word processors and spreadsheets, these kinds of numbers are appropriate. However, for emerging markets, such as the Internet browser market, they make no sense. You need "leading edge" numbers. That's why I commissioned a totally independent survey on browsers from an independent market research company. And the large Microsoft check that I signed in no way compromised their independence...This MR group polled over 10,000 calls to Microsoft and found that "over 95% of those callers were considering using Microsoft Internet Explorer 4.0"! Wow! Look out Marc!

SUNDAY, OCTOBER 12

This is the kind of stuff I have to deal with from those uppity Europeans...

> Mr. Gates:
> I am twenty-two, I speak thirteen different languages fluently, I used to be a pianist at home (Europe), but have decided that I did not like my profession, and am now seriously considering a combined M.D./Ph.D. program in neurolinguistics. How much smarter do you think you are than I?
>
> Respectfully, Mattea De L. S.

Well, Matt old buddy, I'd guess about $40 billion (give or take a few billion) smarter...(And that's not counting Corbis, Teledesic, or any of my secret accounts in Switzerland!) Gee, that's great.

"640K ought to be enough for anybody." BILL GATES

MONDAY, OCTOBER 13

COLUMBUS DAY / THANKSGIVING DAY (CANADA)

Had a great Mexican meal this evening with Melinda. Boy, is she a great cook! And, boy, do those

Mexicans know food! What a great nation! Fantastic food, gorgeous women (although slightly on the hairy side), and an incredible breeding ground for hotshot programming dudes. Our very own Charles Simonyi, chief architect (after me, of course) of Excel, Word, and Word's thesaurus is a Mexican (and one of my best friends). He studied at the University of Mexico City (a real fine school) and his groundbreaking 1976 paper, "Meta-Programming: A Software Production Method," was based upon the ancient systems of meta-bean-farming practiced in his home country. God bless Mexico. (And America, of course.)

TUESDAY, OCTOBER 14

Dr. Pop reports: Madonna's bouncing baby Lola Terra del Fuego hits the big first birthday today. Now we can talk about babies AND the Internet! (And Princess Jennifer can have someone to play chess with.)

I was just joking about the Swiss bank accounts, OK? I've got the Justice Department on my case already. The last thing I need is the IRS, too...

WEDNESDAY, OCTOBER 15

Today, I discovered a rival to Brad Silverberg in the brownnoser of the month contest. Nice try, Rich!

Mr. Gates:

I loved reading your book. It was so interesting to read. It is hot!!! I am glad to hear that Microsoft is growing and making better products. CON-GRATULATIONS and HAPPY BIRTHDAY!!! I am happy for you. Well, all I can say is that I loved your book and I watch every interview I can. Keep up the good work, Mr. Gates. Oh yeah, nice house!!!

Rich L.

Hey, Rich, you want a job at Microsoft? I need guys like you around me.

I'm often asked to describe what animal I think Microsoft would be. Pretty stupid question (as usual!) but I have to humor journalists even though I firmly believe in the old adage "Those who can, do; those who can't, teach; and those who think they can—but can't—become journalists." I usually reply that Microsoft is like an elephant—huge and power-ful yet gentle, sensitive, and intelligent.

I guess the problem with being an elephant is that there are always gnats and flies buzzing around...but at least you have a huge trunk to swat them with...

FRIDAY, OCTOBER 17

Like that pesky little Netscape company... But who cares? What, me worry? Our business model works even if all Internet software is free. Netscape doesn't look very good, but we're still selling Operating Systems...

One of the things I love about working at Microsoft is the people. It's just so cool being surrounded by such powerful, creative, smart individuals. Some of the best brains in America. In fact, I'm sure there must be one or two that are nearly as smart as me. And boy, have these guys got their fingers right on the pulse. Always one step ahead of the (rapidly dwindling) competition. Always knowing every detail of our entire corporate strategy for the coming years. It's cool...

SATURDAY, OCTOBER 18

Those press guys are at it again. Freedom of speech is great (well, except for totally untrue, slanderous, and morally reprehensible stuff...like that UNOFFICIAL Bill Diary thing). Freedom of the press is great, in principle anyway. But freedom of the press to drag all kinds of skeletons and dark secrets out of my closet? I don't think so. I've made some mistakes in the past, done and said some things I've come to regret. I'm human, right? I was young and inexperienced. I was finding out what's right and wrong in life. It's just not fair when they drag my misdemeanors out into the open. We ALL make mistakes. OK, I know I once wrote, "I believe that OS/2 is destined to be the most important operating system, and possibly program, of all time." And I know that I'm obviously way too smart to believe that. But it's a guy thing, right? Basically, if you've got testicles and a johnson, you're sometimes economical with the truth. It's just our nature, we can't help it. We're from Mars, right?

SUNDAY, OCTOBER 19

You know, I really am a babe magnet extraordinaire. Intelligence, self-confidence, enormous bank balance, and killer looks! And my self-deprecating sense of humor...And my awesome personal philosophy: stiff your partners and own the world!

Went down to Barnes & Noble. Bought fifty copies of *The Road Ahead*. One for every bedroom ("Provided by the Friends of Bill Gates Society"). Yeaaaaahhhhhh!

Forgot about the bathrooms. Went back and bought another fifty copies.

And twenty more: one in each Ferrari.

Man, I am THIS cool.

"I think there is a world market for maybe five computers."

THOMAS WATSON, IBM

MONDAY, OCTOBER 20

Sometimes I feel I should just keep my mouth firmly shut. When you're as famous as I am, everything you say gets taken out of context and quoted all over the place. It's just so depressing to see journalists try to rearrange my sentences to mean completely new things. What can I do? Take, for example, "There won't be anything we won't say to people to try and convince them that our way is the way to go." I never, never said that. I wouldn't say something like that. Never. It's just not in my nature. Surely everyone knows that by now.

On the other hand, sometimes I produce such a pearl of wisdom that it's totally satisfying to see it in print. I've been quoted as saying, "If you don't know what you need Windows NT for, you don't need it." I certainly don't know what I need it for.

TUESDAY, OCTOBER 21

Checked out the latest Microsoft quarterly financials. Awesome, as usual. Is there no stopping me? (Trick question. Of course there's no stopping me!)

They say my ego is huge, but that can't be right...I'm not even the highest paid person at Microsoft. Bob Herbold, our COO, gets way more than me! Maybe I should have a quiet word with our Compensation Committee?

WEDNESDAY, OCTOBER 22

Can it be true that the United States government thinks I'm a bullying billionaire with compulsive monopolist tendencies who's out to crush anyone or anything who stands in my way? THAT'S THE STUPIDEST F***ING THING I'VE EVER HEARD!!

THURSDAY, OCTOBER 23

What a month it's been! I'm just soooo busy! Phew! I get tired just thinking about it! Not even had much time to play 'n' learn with Baby Jennifer. According to her mom, she's now adding to the class libraries in MFC. That's my girl.

Got this anonymous e-mail today:

> Bill, is it true that if you use a word processor other than Microsoft Word, you'll eventually go blind?
>
> a WordPerfect developer, Utah

Yes. (Hey, I thought you guys had all left by now...)

FRIDAY, OCTOBER 24

UNITED NATIONS DAY

I really do believe that the information highway has finally become an integral part of my life. I deeply resent it when a piece of information I need is not available via the network. (You can tell I'm smart because I can use "via" correctly in a sentence.) My mountain bike had a flat today, and I spent ages hunting through all my stuff, looking for the repair manual. Boy, was I annoyed! Since it's a book, I could have misplaced it (and did). It obviously should be an interactive, electronic document...always on-line, always available.

SATURDAY, OCTOBER 25

Went out to buy a new bike.

SUNDAY, OCTOBER 26

DAYLIGHT SAVING TIME ENDS

Boy, that extra hour in bed made all the difference this morning! Melinda says (as usual) that I am a raging love beast...Yeahhhhhh! Maybe this time it'll be a boy, ha, ha.

Jeez. Everyone thinks that just because I'm consolidating my on-line strategy by making a couple of deals with a couple of other people, I'm admitting that I can't do it all on my own. Well, it just ain't true. Everyone knows my policy on deals, partners, and joint ventures: "If you can't beat 'em, join 'em... then beat 'em."

Just joking. No really. Just a cheap laugh. A partner is for life—just ask Melinda. And anyway, read the small print in the contract.

"I think they'd kill us in our sleep and sell our organs if the return on investment was good." DILBERT

MONDAY, OCTOBER 27

What do I really want for my birthday tomorrow? Here's my Top Ten Birthday Wish List:

1.   Marc Andreessen's head on a platter.

2.   Cindy Crawford singing "Happy Birthday." (After all, Marilyn's dead, and I'm better looking than JFK.)

3.   A Slinky (made from platinum, of course).

4.   Netscape's collapse due to a catastrophic bug in Navigator (or Communicator, or whatever it's called today).

5. A decent version of Microsoft Bob.

6. The electronic rights to *Sports Illustrated* swimsuit edition.

7. *The Catcher in the Rye* talking book.

8. Microsoft stock price hike to $250 a share.

9. A new pair of Gap khakis, and a Cutter & Buck polo shirt with Microsoft logo.

10. World peace. (And I mean that sincerely, folks.)

TUESDAY, OCTOBER 28

BILL GATES DAY

It's my forty-second birthday! And still boyishly handsome in a rich, hip dude kind of way. (No wonder the babes dig me.) Happy birthday to me! (And happy birthday John Romero—I still look just as young and hip as the Doom-meister!) And what do you get the man who has everything? Melinda gave me a check for $100 with the helpful advice to "spend it on anything you like"...I wouldn't mind, but it was drawn on our joint account. Her heart's in the right place, I guess, but she doesn't quite have the big picture, does she?

She also thinks I should get a proper physical—the guy equivalent of the 100,000 mile service... I kinda agree with her: In principle, I'm as anti–

prostate cancer as the next guy. But I can't bear the thought of some doctor being able to make cocktail-party talk for the next fifty years by virtue of having had his finger in the "thirty-eight billion dollar output port." Uh-uh...No way, Jose...

WEDNESDAY, OCTOBER 29

Are they STILL talking about NTW/NTS? All this stuff is getting on my nerves. Any excuse to attack me and my company. The crux of this issue is that NT Workstation and NT Server are two totally different products intended for two totally different functions. I'll admit that they use identical kernels, but there's much more difference than some simple registry settings. Those registry settings directly result in forty-eight run-time variable changes, which, in turn, cascade down to result in over 700 key operational value differences. This is not trivial stuff. And if you change the registry settings yourself, you'll get totally unpredictable results, even though, initially, it looks like you've gotten one product to look like the other. And the performance hit will be terrible.

I mean, we did over a billion dollars in server revenue. With the price difference between the two—maybe $800—one of them costs 35% of what the other does. So a billion dollars goes to $350 million...Like I said, the performance hit will be terrible.

THURSDAY, OCTOBER 30

HONESTLY, there are WAY more differences between NTW and NTS than $800 and a few registry settings...

1. The packaging is totally different, and...

2. Er...loads of other stuff...and...

3. If you get NTW and hack it to be a server, you'll have broken your license agreement and I'LL SUE YOUR ASS OFF!

FRIDAY, OCTOBER 31

HALLOWEEN

Tried to dress Baby Jennifer as a baby Borg for Halloween, but Melinda wasn't having any of it. "JUST USE THE BUNNY EARS, OKAY! For such a smart man you can be so UNBELIEVABLY STUPID!" Man, that was way harsh. So I took Jennifer into the office for an hour with her bunny ears. She's just SO cute. You know, for a subset, she really is totally adorable. I don't want to blow my Microsoft street cred, but I LOVE that girl...

SATURDAY, NOVEMBER 1

I just have to laugh when the PC mags complain about us releasing applications too early. Guess what landed on my desk this morning? *PC Computing*...February issue. I rest my case.

And while I'm setting the record straight about the PC press, anyone who reviewed the latest Encarta and Cinemania and claimed that there's nothing particularly new or original should call the pope—and ask him why he doesn't issue radically new yearly updates. If it ain't broke, don't fix it.

SUNDAY, NOVEMBER 2

I've had a while to experience the joys of fatherhood, so I believe I'm qualified to come up with my Gates Baby Specification Top Ten:

1. Two hours between recharges

2. Infinite capacity removable storage

3. EnergyStar shutdown (nonprogrammable)

4. SCSI port

5. Multiple registry entries

6. Compact laptop design

7. Plug and Play accessories

8. Small footprint

9. Software-only audio controls

10. Bidirectional cereal port

Sounds about right to me.

"Love is a better master than duty." ALBERT EINSTEIN

MONDAY, NOVEMBER 3

Decided to pick Encarta for one of my routine, random quality checks. (Microsoft TQM for zero defect software.) Is it as totally comprehensive and all-encompassing as we claim? I pick, utterly at random, Altair, elephant, Apple, IBM, and *The Catcher in the Rye*...

Plenty on the Altair (hmmmm, halcyon days) with some real neat video of me and Paul standing outside Harvard, clutching THAT issue of *Popular Electronics.*

Plenty on elephants, and most other mammals...

Plenty on apples, and most other fruits, food, and drink...

A line on IBM, in the Ancient History section...

And *The Catcher in the Rye* in its entirety...with clips from the 1974 movie of the same name starring a youthful John Travolta as Holden...

TUESDAY, NOVEMBER 4

ELECTION DAY

A whole year in office, and already a nice tax cut so I'll only have to pay 20% on my $40 billion. Cool! Nice work, Bill #2!

Here's my list of the Top Ten Reasons to Run for President:

1. I want to buy an old Cessna, paint it flashy colors, and call it Air Force 98.

2. Gennifer Flowers will want me too.

3. I have way more money than Steve Forbes.

4. Then I can fire Janet Reno and close the Justice Department.

5. Warren Buffett can be Secretary of the Treasury.

6. As head of Microsoft, I only have 4,000 people kissing my ass.

7. I'm much better looking than Ross Perot.

8. Microsoft Money would be great for balancing the budget.

9. I could make sure THREE things are certain: death, taxes, and Windows 98.

10. It would be way cool to be president of two big thingies.

WEDNESDAY, NOVEMBER 5

OK, so sometimes I'm not too popular in certain quarters. And I do have a bad rep in the press for my anti-...er, I mean highly...competitive approach. But

I'm a basically good person: I'm always doing great work for charity...It's just that I don't like to talk about it.

But on the other hand, you should know about "Libraries Online," my philanthropic initiative to help library systems in economically disadvantaged communities provide public access to the Internet (and IE!) and multimedia personal computers (with Windows and Encarta!). Boy, what a great guy I am!

THURSDAY, NOVEMBER 6

Why don't we have any "glamour" products? I don't understand it. Some of these companies are making major bucks! Should we be leaving this money on the table? Microsoft Babes. Hmmm. That has a certain ring to it. Or an MS-SI joint venture on the swimsuit issue? I could interview the models as part of the selection process. Huh, hu-hu, huh...

FRIDAY, NOVEMBER 7

Who wants to be in the book business? It's boring. Books are things of the past—we're moving on to new form factors. Think "bits" not "atoms"...

Baited Nathan Myhrvold today by saying: "Don't you find the math in *A Brief History of Time* too simple? I know I do," and "So, is it true that Stephen Hawking didn't think you were smart enough to stay at Cambridge then?" and "I don't know how technical you are, but being an assistant chef must be much less intellectually stressful for you."

It's strange how, as time passes, language adapts and the meanings of certain words change. When everyone says that IE4 is "really cool" they don't mean it's at a low temperature. Rather, they mean that it's cleverly constructed, very useful, and much better than Navigator. Cool!

And when they say that working at Microsoft is "wicked" they don't mean doing bad stuff for the antichrist, they mean that it's a very pleasurable (in a free-soda kind of way) and enriching (in a lots-of-Microsoft-options kind of way) experience.

And when Microsoft says "Beta Version" we don't mean the prerelease buggy version being tested on the unsuspecting public. No. We mean the release version software being given away for free in order to destroy the competition! Way cool! And wicked!

Similarly, authorship is a strange and ever shifting concept. After all, those great plays by that Shakespeare guy probably weren't written by him at all. He just wrote a couple of best-sellers to get his revenue going, then licensed works from up-and-coming writers and put his name on them. But it's still fine to say that Shakespeare wrote them because the concepts were probably his...and he did all the marketing.

So, in a way, Paul Allen and I really DID write MS-DOS. (I believe one of our brochures does actually say this. A big "thank you" to Tim Patterson.)

"The world is not just
about movies, movies,
and more movies."

NICHOLAS NEGROPONTE

MONDAY, NOVEMBER 10

And while I'm on the subject of DOS, do I care if Granddad-from-Hell has made the code for PC-DOS public domain and released it onto the Internet? Talk about closing the stable door after the horse has bolted! I realize that you're a little bitter, Ray, but really, it's not dignified. And you're STILL suing me? Well, I'm shaking in my boots. Really scared. NOT!

And talking of loser operating systems, I've been reading more sad articles about how Unix really will beat Windows NT, because now it's FREE (in the form of Linux). AS IF!

OK, so there are a couple of million manic computer geeks out there writing OS software for free.

And using the Internet as the ultimate marketing vehicle…Free downloads, a bug here, a bug there, get the users to subsidize the Quality Assurance Department with their monetary contributions and their bug reports…Hey, now THAT really sounds really familiar…(And, hey, even I can't get my programmers working for free. This is unfair competition: surely the Justice Department will want to look into this?)

Read my lips: EVERYONE wants Windows. Don't they?

TUESDAY, NOVEMBER 11

VETERANS DAY / REMEMBRANCE DAY (CANADA)

Hey! Cool! Judge Zobel posted his ruling in the Louise Woodward baby death case on the Net first—making Internet history. So us Web-aware, techno-savvy types knew the news before ANYONE else! Yeah, right. The traffic was so heavy that no one could get on the site…I had to watch CNN instead. Maybe Ted Turner isn't so dumb after all.

WEDNESDAY, NOVEMBER 12

I can't help but think that, in some ways, people have it all wrong about me when they refer to me as America's richest man. OK, so I have a current net worth in excess of $40 billion, but they don't realize that this is PAPER wealth. A correction in the Microsoft stock price would slash this value. And as the major Microsoft stockholder, I can't sell any substantial amount of my stock without causing a major loss of market confidence...I bet if I tried to sell all my stock today and retire, I'd barely make $22 billion. And then there's taxes of around $7 billion. Hey, what can a guy do with just $15 billion?

THURSDAY, NOVEMBER 13

On the other hand, maybe I'll just cash in, liquidate, and live on a boat somewhere. There's nothing worse than a billionaire who doesn't know how to relax. Ha, ha.

Hey, Apple! Looks like I saved your ass yet again, huh? IE4 is now available for Macintosh users! It's true! All the good stuff comes from Microsoft...

FRIDAY, NOVEMBER 14

On the other, other hand (ha, ha) if you sit still, the value of what you have drops to zero pretty damn quickly. I can't afford to start thinking about taking it easy. If I don't crush THEM, they'll be coming to get ME...

Ralph Nader (at his anti-Microsoft conference) is still bitching about me today...What a loser! How can he claim that consumers are being damaged by Microsoft? Thanks to me, the cost of computing has fallen 10 million–fold since I invented the micro-processor in 1971. That's the equivalent of getting a Boeing 747 for the price of a copy of Money 98! If this innovation had been applied to automobiles, a new car would cost about two dollars and it would travel at the speed of sound and go 600 miles on a thimble of gas. (And it would come preloaded with Windows CE—but, hey, that's another story.)

I would have liked to have gone and presented my side…but participating in this kind of hostile en-vironment would be like walking into an ambush with sharpshooters on every hilltop. And why would I want to sit there and listen to two days of Microsoft bashing? (I can just go to a DoJ hearing for that.)

SATURDAY, NOVEMBER 15

Arrived in Vegas for the Comdex show…I played a quick round of golf with Mirage multi-millionaire Steve Wynn. Hey, sometimes you gotta mix with the poor people.

I love playing golf. It's the walking around out-side part I hate.

Melinda went wild on the slot machines. I couldn't get her to stop. "But I want us to be rich" she kept saying. Gee, honey, I guess I better try harder.

Today I gave my Comdex Fall Keynote Address. And boy, was I good. I had the audience eating out of my hand...I've certainly come a long way since 1985, when I first had a chance to do a keynote here. At that time, I had my dad come down and change the slides for me. And the only thing I worried about was the condensation on the slides, whether they would dry out properly or not. I think we're all lucky to be working in this field. We're providing tools that empower people to do their best.

Hit the *PC Computing* MVP ("Microsoft Valuable Product") Awards. The usual raft of accolades for Office, Word, Excel, Access, Publisher, FrontPage, IE, NT, Visual Basic, Internet Information Server...We rule!

After all that excitement I had a tough time getting to sleep. Luckily I was able to read a copy of *Slate,* and soon dropped off. (Sorry, Michael.)

"The best way to predict the future is to invent it." ALAN KAY

MONDAY, NOVEMBER 17

Went around the Comdex show floor and counted the handheld PCs based on Windows CE.

I'm just so cool! The Newton was a neat idea. Nice try, Apple! But with WinCE, the time of the personal organizer has arrived. The handheld PC was a critical milestone in our continuing strategy to...well, sell even more copies of Windows, actually. Cooool!

Inducted into the Computer Reseller News Hall of Fame. What an honor! Who says advertising doesn't work?

TUESDAY, NOVEMBER 18

And shows are a great opportunity to check out the competition. Just one problem...Do I have any competition? In fact, the only competition I have left is from Sun, Oracle, and Netscape. But are they serious competitors?

Sun builds workstations, but pins its hopes on Java. People don't want workstations, they want PCs (to the tune of about sixty million per year). And certainly no one makes money creating languages. (Not even me.)

Oracle thinks they can create a low-cost network computer. But it's predicated on people wanting less features in their PC. Not likely. The whole PC revolution is founded on personal empowerment.

And finally there's little Netscape. With nothing but a free browser and a hot IPO on the back of Internet mania. We can embrace and extend. We can keep making money (from operating systems, at least) even if all Internet software is free.

The reality is this: Game over. I win. Yeaaahhhh!

We also showed Windows 98—the major new release of our flagship consumer OS. We've invested
nearly three years of development time and over
25,000 hours of usability testing to deliver the new
capabilities our customers have requested. It rocks!
And think of the upgrade revenue! Yeaaaahhhh!

Shows are always a good time to catch up on my
e-mail, and to surf the Web for useful and interesting
new sites. Guess what I found? More sick, twisted
anti-Bill stuff...I thought I'd found the worst with
that morally reprehensible and outrageous fiction,
that Secret Diary thing. But it gets worse. Here's a
Boycott Microsoft site. (Note to lawyer: surely this is
a restraint of trade?)

What is it with these people? I am wise, I am
good, I am Bill. And Microsoft is the world's best-
loved software corporation. (We must be. We're the
biggest.)

Maybe our games strategy isn't so bad...Win-
dows 98 really does give those hardcore gamers some
serious advantages. All those Quake freaks are dying
to be able to play a game AND be able to receive a
fax in the background...Or be able to hit a button
and go over and look at something else...Anyway,

I'm too busy to do code and stuff. While in Vegas, I'm having lunch with Gillian Anderson's agent to discuss her fee for doing voice-overs for another crucial Microsoft product I'm just about to think of. Huh, hu-hu, huh...

FRIDAY, NOVEMBER 21

Man, I love these Comdex parties. Went out on the town with some other high-tech dudes for a few beers. Here's my Top Ten Things You'll Only Do When You're Drunk...

1. Dance like John Travolta in *Saturday Night Fever*. And bump into things. And break them. And not give a damn about it.

2. Try to sleep with your wife's best friend in the marketing group.

3. Make yourself a delicious snack of French's mustard and stale Wonder Bread.

4. Decide that the printer paper tray would look better on your head.

5. Decide to walk back to the hotel, even though it's seven miles away and you have a limo waiting anyway.

6. Moon Stewart Alsop.

7. Decide that you and Ann Winblad really should be together.

8. AutoDial every woman in your electronic organizer (running Windows CE, natch!) at 2:00 A.M. and say, "Hi, I was just thinking about you. Maybe we should meet up. Now-ish..."

9. Fall asleep on the stairs, with your Gap pants around your ankles.

10. Get into a fight with the limo driver.

11. Attempt to sleep with any woman who shows the slightest interest in your billions.

12. Get really emotional, put on the most morose record in the jukebox, and weep about the good old days when Apple, Lotus, and Novell were still a force to be reckoned with.

13. Make lots of inadvisable bets. Like Navigator being down to 10% market share in the next year.

14. Throw people, fully clothed, into the pool (just for old times sake).

15. Say, "I love you, man!" to Marc Andreessen and Steve Jobs.

OK, Top Fifteen...I guess I had a pretty full evening!

SATURDAY, NOVEMBER 22

Man, I feel bad. The combination of greasy food and lots of beer isn't a good one...I spent most of the night on the MAPI—Man and Porcelain Interface.

I told you I was a role model! Well, here's even more proof: an e-mail from Brian, age eight, Albuquerque...

Dear Mr. Gates:
I need to dress like you for a school presentation. Any fashion tips?

I used to button my top button, and it took me a while to figure out that that wasn't cool. So you'd better watch out for that one. And don't forget to brush your teeth and comb your hair (never the other way around).

SUNDAY, NOVEMBER 23

Checked out this year's *Upside* magazine 100— their list of movers and shakers in our little industry... This year they've split the list into ten Top Tens to give more losers a chance of being #1 in something. Isn't that sweet? But we all know that the REAL list is the Top Ten TITANS...But how come I'm only #2? What does Andy Grove have that I haven't? Apart from Intel?

AND STEVE JOBS DOESN'T EVEN MAKE THE TOP TEN! LOSER!

"I never miss a chance to have sex or appear on television."

GORE VIDAL

MONDAY, NOVEMBER 24

Looks like Andy Warhol was wrong. Some people get thirty minutes. Like me. Yeaaaahhhhhh!

Yikes! How did the DoJ get hold of that Top Secret Internal Memo? I thought we'd burned it! Jim thinks we should "leverage our Windows monopoly" by bundling our Web browser to help us "win" against Netscape. He adds, helpfully, "The current path is to simply copy everything that Netscape does packaging and product wise." Does this loser still have a job?

TUESDAY, NOVEMBER 25

Check this out! Microsoft Greetings Workshop with Internet delivery functionality... Now I'm bringing Web authoring to children, bored housewives, and stupid people! I'll send Marc Andreessen a complimentary copy!

I hear that Philip K. Dick wrote some of his novels using the *I Ching*. I too like to consult the mystical bamboo tiles when I get stuck writing tight, sharp code.

WEDNESDAY, NOVEMBER 26

I got a Christmas mailing this morning from *Encyclopaedia Britannica* trying to sell me their whole thing on...Wait for it...CD-ROM! I guess Encarta must be really hurting them now. But at least they're getting a little aggressive. It'd be no fun destroying them without them at least putting up something of a fight.

But I don't think they've quite got the idea... They're offering a heavily discounted, competitive-upgrade style scheme—just return the "CD-ROM encyclopaedia that came with your computer" in the reply-paid envelope...I decided to take advantage of this and so I hunted for my copy of Encarta and tried to return it to them. Except I couldn't. It won't fit in the reply-paid envelope! Ha-ha! I guess they're not putting up a fight after all...

THURSDAY, NOVEMBER 27

THANKSGIVING DAY

Day off. Even at Microsoft.

Well I was here, but where was everyone else? Two days off just to eat some turkey? Sheesh...

I get to spend the day snooping through Steve Ballmer's e-mail (that's how I make sure I always have the inside scoop). And guess what I found? A begging e-mail from that guy who used to run that PagePlus company! A former president of some insignificant software company that I successfully crushed! Yeaaahhhh! Life is good!

> Hi, Steve!
> I know you're busy, but I thought you might have a job for me . . . I was the founder and CEO of Serif, a dinky little corporation (around $10 million) that developed and marketed PagePlus, a dinky little Publisher competitor. Serif was sold recently, and my services are no longer required. So I'm looking for a job. Got one? Please.
> Sincerely, Gwyn J.

This should amuse Melinda. Perhaps we could get him a job on Bob—the Microsoft equivalent of the Siberian salt mines.

SATURDAY, NOVEMBER 29

I think Steve's on the same track (fortunately for HIM). He replied:

> From: Steve B.
> Nothing obvious but will keep it in mind, loser...

SUNDAY, NOVEMBER 30

I had a cozy breakfast at home today with Melinda and Baby Jennifer. The new pad is SO cool. Lots of glass so we can sit inside and look out over Lake Washington, while the sun shines down on us. Beautiful. Life is good.

But then some tourist boat—filled with poor people, I guess—sails by. And they're all looking in at me! Hey, builder dudes! For $50 million, don't I get one-way glass? Or at least a few blinds?

Apparently, those Brits have decided to rename Heathrow Airport as Princess Diana Airport. That's pretty cool...But not as cool as people flying into Seattle's Bill Gates Airport. AWESOME! I'm gonna make it happen...

"I guess I don't so much mind being old as I mind being fat and old." PETER GABRIEL

MONDAY, DECEMBER 1

I've been thinking. And, for a change, not about the computer biz. I've come to the conclusion that what we all call "stress" is really "adrenaline addiction." This is the idea that we use intensity (in any form—fear, anger, excitement, the Internet, crushing one's competitors) to repress deeper underlying feelings of loss, abandonment, and disconnection. It certainly explains a lot...

I now have one of those "My Other Car Is a..." stickers for my Lexus. Of course, mine does not continue "...Porsche" but, instead, reads "...Fleet of Twenty Ferraris." Supercool!

TUESDAY, DECEMBER 2

More work on my Top Ten lists. This time it's my list of the Top Operating Systems Ever...

1. **Windows NT**
2. **Windows 98**
3. **Windows 95**
4. **Windows CE**
5. **Windows 3.1**
6. **MS-DOS** (all versions)
7. Erghhh...
8. **The Human Body!**
9. There aren't any more...

Great news for Corel! WordPerfect Suite 8 is the world's best-selling software product ever!

Based upon sales through the Egghead retail chain's Dallas store. On a Sunday. Between 2:00 and 3:00. Not including Windows sales. Or Flight Simulator.

Yep, that's a real best-seller!

Read my Scorpio horoscope for this week. It says, "Individual inventors and entrepreneurs will continue to dominate the business spotlight as more conventional institutions struggle to keep up." Yup, like Corel! Even the stars love me...

Breakfast with the big M... Now she wants our technology-showcase home to feature her latest addition to her conceptual range of "simply interactive" household appliances connected to the information highway. It's the Simply Interactive Toilet, or SIT...

Powered by the latest Intel Pentium with MMX—"Intel Underneath"—the SIT (is this a thin client or a fat one?) will e-mail or page the home owner whenever it needs the attention of a plumber, or when the toilet paper level reaches a preset minimum. And it'll save on costly and painful medical treatment by carrying out (using built-in video technology) instant medical examinations while you read *The Road Ahead* (have you bought your copy yet?). If a cream or ointment is needed then the SIT—using Microsoft AutoMap—will supply directions to the nearest CVS. Melinda...stick to babies, OK? Duh!

FRIDAY, DECEMBER 5

Andy (from Intel—who else?) called me today to chat about the computer biz. "Thank God," he said, "that we live in a society that is so gullible that it will accept any standard pushed onto them by true visionaries like ourselves..." Yeeeeaaahhhh! I'll see you tomorrow, Andy, for the usual game of "Kick the Peasant"!

SATURDAY, DECEMBER 6

Larry! This network computer idea is just so stooooopid! Networks will be overloaded if PCs go diskless. The cost of the server will go up, a lot more than the cost of the disks would. And no one wants to work with less powerful, less funky PCs. Well, that's just my humble opinion. I might be wrong. And if I am wrong (which, of course, I won't be), at least I've got the NetPC in reserve. And the Windows Terminal. And WebTV. Hee, hee, hee...

And Larry, what have YOU got in reserve? Apple? Hee, hee, hee...

These new Internet Assistants for Microsoft Excel, Word, and PowerPoint are just something else. You can use them to create home pages on the World Wide Web. All you have to do is download the tools from our Web site. When you save a document, choose HTML format, and it's ready to post on the Web. You can also use Microsoft Word to communicate more clearly through e-mail or the Internet. Create your message inside Word, using its formatting options like italic, bold, indented paragraphs, and bulleted lists to emphasize your point. Then send the message without ever closing Word. Hmmmm... This would make great copy for a Microsoft Office ad. I'll e-mail marketing right away. Uh...how do I e-mail direct from Word, again?

Melinda says I am a raging love beast. I know, babe...

"Common sense is genius dressed in its working clothes."

RALPH WALDO EMERSON

Check out Internet World in sunny New York for more about IE4 and our continuing Net domination strategy..."We delivered on all our promises, and way more. We've shipped our world-class Internet Explorer 4.0 on four different platforms. And we kicked Netscape's butt!" Yeahhhhh!

Cindy Crawford's agent wants me to talk to Cindy about computers and the Internet. Right. She wants me bad.

TUESDAY, DECEMBER 9

Melinda made me breakfast today. We sat, read the papers, and discussed business. Sometimes she can be OK.

Quiet day with my PC. Went trolling for chicks on the Net. They didn't believe I was THE Bill. Except for this...

> From: Alissa C.
> I think that Bill Gates is a wonder and a marvel
> ...irresistibly cute, even without the money.
> Really. Is this normal?

Absolutely, babe. Except for the money bit...

WEDNESDAY, DECEMBER 10

During the development of Windows 98, the team gave birth to seventy-two kids, drank 3,410,680 cans of (free) soda, and ate enough pizza to cover the Microsoft Campus three times over. That's the kind of information I have at MY fingertips...but I'm not a control freak. Oh, no. I just believe that knowledge is power.

And I guess that money is power, too.

I had to laugh today. I was talking by video-link with some guys in one of our "developing-market" territories (the United Kingdom, actually). I'd assumed that they were only a couple of years behind us in terms of technology but it's much worse than I had ever imagined...Apparently, their terrestrial TV has only just started showing *The Lone Ranger*! And they're scheduled to start on series one of *The X-Files* and *The Simpsons* in 2011! No wonder we're not selling much over there...

Constantly reassessing my plans and priorities is one of the keys to my amazing ability to adapt to changing circumstances and new competitors. So here's my Top Ten Priorities (for the next few weeks):

1. Dominate the Internet.

2. Get big in education.

3. Do more cool games.

4. Buy more content.

5. Er...

6. Get laid.

7. Er, there aren't any more.

My great buddy Andy Grove, over at Intel, claims that a microprocessor manufacturing plant only costs $2.5 billion to open. Maybe one would make the perfect garden ornament for the new house! I'd better get it sorted soon though, because Andy claims that the cost will soon rise to $10 billion...

Hey, entrepreneurs! Here's a great business opportunity...Just buy a couple of microprocessor manufacturing plants, then sell them to Intel next year. That's what I call real return on investment!

Browse through four-hundred-year-old manuscripts deep in a European library. Run a meeting where six people draw on the same white board at the same time, even though none of them are in the same room. Read an electronic book where the illustrations move, the charts evolve, and the footnotes come alive. At Microsoft, I've always known the PC would deliver this kind of access—access that opens up the most exciting possibilities in the world. And now the Internet expands these possibilities more than ever. Good job I invented it, eh? Yeaahhhh!

"There's no control of look and feel." BILL GATES

MONDAY, DECEMBER 15

Today I had a high-powered end-of-year review meeting with Steve Ballmer and Nathan Myhrvold. It was pretty tense.

Just before lunch, we hear Steve emitting a beeping noise. "Oh, that's my emergency beeper," he says and lifts his watch to his ear and talks into the end of his tie. After the call, he notices that we're staring at him, and he explains: "It's my new emergency communication system: I have an earpiece built into my watch and a microphone sewn into the end of my tie. That way, I can take a call anywhere." Impressive.

Anyway, we continue, but five minutes later, the meeting is again interrupted. This time it's Nathan beeping. "Hey, this must be an emergency," he says, taps his earlobe, and begins talking into thin air. When he's finished, he sees me and Steve are staring at HIM and he explains: "I also have an emergency communication system. But my earpiece is actually implanted in my earlobe, and the microphone is actually embedded in this fake tooth. Our future products group is doing some really good stuff, huh?" Pretty neat.

So we continue. Five minutes later, I decide to go for it...and I let off this thunderous fart! Steve and Nathan look at me in shock, and I say: "Uhh, guys, get me a piece of paper...I'm receiving a fax." That showed them! Yeaaaahhhhh!

TUESDAY, DECEMBER 16

Did you know that all proceeds from my book *The Road Ahead,* first published back in 1995, have gone to fund technology projects in twenty-three schools around the United States? Well over $4 million has been donated to provide access to technology, training, and support for community-based school programs nationwide. *The Road Ahead* program is administered by the National Foundation for the Improvement of Education (NFIE) in Washington, D.C.

And what a great Christmas present! Your wife/ husband, children, friends, and small furry creatures will be delighted! Order your copy (paperback, by Bill Gates, Nathan Myhrvold, Peter Rinearson) from Amazon.com for just $11.16 (you save: $4.79 or 30%).

I'm a good guy, really.

WEDNESDAY, DECEMBER 17

Of course, that $4 million is dwarfed by the $50 million I've spent on my house (a 40,000-square-foot waterfront palace, along the east bank of Lake Washington, just south of the 520 bridge). But a guy has to live somewhere, right?

So, now you know where that $89 that you paid for Windows 95 went. I bet you feel good now...

THURSDAY, DECEMBER 18

But it's only a house. For $30 million you could get...a book! Three years ago I was lucky enough to be able to buy Leonardo da Vinci's *Codex Leicester*. Yes, it's a book (of about seventy pages). But not just any book...Like myself, Leonardo was the foremost genius of his time (we really have a lot in common) and this manuscript combines drawings and text to touch on almost the whole of nature, and reveals Leonardo as a man of transcendent brilliance. (That has a nice ring to it, don't you think?)

FRIDAY, DECEMBER 19

Dear Santa:

I know it's early, but here's what I need for Christmas...

1. Gap khakis

2. A new Lexus coupe, in metallic gray

3. An issue of *Slate* with naked chicks,
   a Gillian Anderson interview, rock 'n' roll
   and video game reviews

4. A walk-on appearance in *Friends*
   (as Jennifer Aniston's new lover)

5. A real, live UFO

6. World peace

Ha-ha! Just kidding about #6!

SATURDAY, DECEMBER 20

I just received an outrageous property tax assessment on my little house. I was just kidding about the gold taps and the *Mona Lisa*! There's no way it's worth $50 million! I bet if I put it on the market today, it wouldn't even fetch half of that. I mean, it's a USED mansion…What can I say? You make a few bucks, and everyone wants to take it off you…

SUNDAY, DECEMBER 21

In the end, I realized that this was not going to be the year of the push-up. They're just SO low-tech! Instead, I bought one of those groovy stationary bikes (using Melinda's credit card again). And best of all, I can read the *Wall Street Journal* while exercising. Now that's what I call multitasking! Coooool...

"Don't let me slow your search for someone who's interested." DOGBERT

CompuServe? Steve Case is welcome to it. I could have bought it, but I figured it was cheaper and easier to ensure MSN's position as the #2 on-line service by letting HIM buy it. And I see that America Online is now claiming 11 million members. Another made-up-number alert!

What should I get Jennifer for Christmas? The complete set of the new Spice Girls dolls? Or the complete Fisher-Price company?

Of course, being the world's richest and most powerful dude, there are those big things that I really, really want for Christmas but that I just know I'm not going to get...So I'll just have to buy them myself...

So here's my Happy Christmas Bill, Love Bill list.

1. Er...I'm the man who has everything, already.

2. Netscape. (Just kidding. Ha!)

3. A night of uninterrupted hot rooting with Melinda. (Hey, I can dream, can't I?)

WEDNESDAY, DECEMBER 24

FIRST DAY OF HANUKKAH

Wow! Guess what the *New York Times* said this morning? Geneticists have INCONTROVERTIBLE (another good word, huh?) evidence that men and women were once separate races, men evolving in Asia and women evolving in Africa. It was simply a coincidence that they were infertile when they met. The clitoris, so goes the speculation in the paper, is the last vestige of the inseminating organ of a conquered, enslaved, trivialized, and finally emasculated race of weaker, but not necessarily dumber, anthropoids! I'm not sure Melinda's going to be too happy about this news. There could be trouble...

THURSDAY, DECEMBER 25

CHRISTMAS DAY

Happy Christmas to me, Melinda, Baby Jennifer, and everyone who knows and loves me.

And, in reviewing my year, what better than my Top Ten List of Microsoft Innovations:

1. The GUI

2. DOS

3. The Internet

4. Drive Doubling

5. C++ and Object orientation

6. The Office Suite

7. MSN. Internet for Everyone

8. BASIC

9. A PC on every desk...

10. And in every home...

11. With a handheld PC in every briefcase...

12. Running Windows

13. OEM

14. The spreadsheet

15. Predatory pricing

16. The preannouncement

17. The word processor

18. Home finance

19. The "Nerd" interview

20. The technology CEO book thing

21. Ruthless competition

22. Competitor crushing

23. Kicking them when they're down

24. Investing in them just to spin it out a bit longer

25. Dancing on their graves

Er, this needs to be a Top 100, at least...

FRIDAY, DECEMBER 26

KWANZA / BOXING DAY (CANADA)

Hmmmm...

From: Dave M.

Neither Bill Gates nor Microsoft invented the GUI. It was invented by Xerox at Xerox PARC (Palo Alto Research Center).

Who cares?

SATURDAY, DECEMBER 27

I've been reflecting about why people hate me so...Number one, it's envy. Surely the fact that I'm the richest guy on the planet has something to do with it, and the fact that my company has grown so consistently for so long a period of time. Also, it is the most visible company attached to the PC revolution, and I think people have a certain amount of free-floating anxiety about what these things are going to do to them and their jobs. It's almost natural that the richest guy who has the most visible company that has been so dominant in so many markets is going to be the object of a great deal of hatred. In fact, it would be surprising if it were to be different. But I can live with it!

SUNDAY, DECEMBER 28

I'm actually quite envious of kids growing up today. They won't have to go through all the things we have gone through. And, in fact, when we look back at today's personal computers, I think we'll say, "Hey, these were the machines that couldn't listen, couldn't talk, couldn't see." The operating system, yes, it will still have a file manager and a multitasking manager in it, but 90% of the code will relate to these new input systems. And so the tools that these kids will have to pursue their curiosity and do new things will be quite amazing.

Problem is, Jennifer STILL can't use her Microsoft EasyBall too well! Where am I going wrong as a parent?

"Just do it." NIKE

MONDAY, DECEMBER 29

Caught up on the hot scientific stuff today. Wow! Apparently, a team of astrophysicists has come up with a new theory on the end of the universe…The good news: it won't collapse back into an infinitely dense speck of matter. The bad news: it will scatter into an infinitely diffuse, pitch-black expanse of nothingness. All the visible lights will go out in 100 trillion years, then all the cinders will burn out in ten trillion trillion trillion years, then all the remaining black holes will decompose into subatomic particles in 10,000 trillion trillion trillion trillion trillion trillion trillion trillion years.

Phew! Looks like I have enough time to achieve complete software and content domination, after all…

TUESDAY, DECEMBER 30

Everyone was in high New Year spirits today. I heard a great joke when I was standing by the photocopier…

Q. What's the difference between Bill Gates and a Rottweiler?

A. A Rottweiler will eventually give up and let go!

Ha-ha-ha! Great joke! I just love the friendly office banter we have at Microsoft! (Note: I must remember to ask Melinda what a Rottweiler is tonight.)

Personally, I've been using the Internet to play bridge, to stay up-to-date on the latest in biotechnology, to buy books, to learn about pregnancy and all the things that go on there...In fact, I'm starting to wonder if Melinda isn't keeping some news from me!

The world is full of superlative events. I reach new extremes. It's incredible. There's some kind of attenuation for past events, so I'm constantly running into the most stupid thing I've ever heard. Makes life fun! I know that my climaxes are ahead of me, not just behind me...New products to steal...er, invent...new markets to dominate...new competitors to crush...What a blast! Roll on New Year!

Are You Like
BILL GATES?
QUIZ

Go on! Do your little self-assessment thing. I found an Are You Like Bill Gates? quiz in one of my old *Software Entrepreneur* magazines. Like one of those *Cosmo* quizzes that Melinda loves so much...I scored pretty good. Now you try...

1. You're shown a Beta of a hot new software product that defines a whole new category. Do you...

___ **A.** Begin preliminary licensing negotiations, then pull out of the deal...but only after you've reverse engineered and prepared a competitive product?

___ **B.** Attempt to buy the company, but get blocked by the FTC?

___ **C.** Do both of the above?

2. You hear that the forthcoming release of a competitive word processor beats the hell out of Microsoft Word. Do you...

___ **A.** Preannounce that the next version of Word does EVERYTHING (and then some) the competitor does, but faster, easier, and more intelligently...and it's out next week?

_____ **B.** Act philosophical? After all, competition breeds great products, right?

_____ **C.** Just laugh? Who cares about features? Nothing is going to shake Word from the top spot. (This one's impossible, but I guess I can suspend disbelief for a moment, hypothetically speaking...)

3. You need a great game to hang the "Windows 95 is a great games platform" flag from. Do you...

_____ **A.** Launch Flight Simulator 13?

_____ **B.** Tie-up with a major developer like EA?

_____ **C.** Panic, and quickly license the first 3D shoot-'em-up that looks a little like Flight Simulator, but with lasers? (Panic? Me? Inconceivable. It was part of my plan, OK?)

4. Microsoft Office is under serious price pressure from SmartSuite and PerfectOffice in the European OEM market. Do you...

_____ **A.** Improve the feature set of MS Office?

_____ **B.** Get down to some serious price negotiations?

_____ **C.** Slash the Gateway and Dell buy prices on Office to virtually zero? After all, no revenue for you is better than ANY revenue for them!

5. Corel buys the WordPerfect family, ready to launch an assault on MS Office. Do you...

____ **A.** Feel smug? After all, you've got a great new version of Office up your corporate sleeve.

____ **B.** Announce that the next version of Office does EVERYTHING the competitor does, but faster, easier, and more intelligently... and it's out next week?

____ **C.** Not even notice?

6. The entire software market shifts from being corporate driven to consumer dominated. Do you...

____ **A.** License, develop, beg, borrow, and steal an enormous range of titles for the home market...get some boring old peripherals, add a marginally novel twist, then brand them ready for those home-user suckers... and do some TV ads with Rolling Stones tunes?

____ **B.** Add "and in every home" to the corporate motto of "On every desk"...get Patty Stonesifer to set up the Consumer Division...then get a wife and kid to support the image of Microsoft as a caring, sharing, '90s kind of company?

____ **C.** Do both of the above?

7. Microsoft is in the unheard of position of generating more revenue from interest on cash in the bank than from sales. Do you...

___ **A.** Worry?

___ **B.** Rock backward and forward, pondering future corporate strategy?

___ **C.** Laugh?
(You have to admit...it IS pretty funny. "Gloat" would be a good word, too.)

8. You completely miss a huge, fundamental change in technology as the market shifts away from personal computing to the Internet. Do you...

___ **A.** Pretend you knew all along? After all, MSN is the "Internet made easy for everyone..."

___ **B.** Rush out a book of your own predictions about how great the Internet will be...buy up as many Internet tools as possible...feel relieved that you bought all that electronic content over the last few years?

___ **C.** Do both of the above?
(Don't forget: Microsoft has an Internet Division!)

9. You launch a strongly branded new operating system with a cute clouds motif, then find that third-party, compatible products are using this motif. Do you...

___ **A.** Think: That's great...It means that consumers can tell what will—and won't—work with the new operating system?

___ **B.** Insist that those third-party guys use a teeny, half-inch-square logo to show consumers compatibility?

___ **C.** Sue the ones with competitive products...ignore the ones without?

10. Home is...

___ **A.** The world's leading, and most strongly recognized, software brand?

___ **B.** A massive underground bunker complete with movie theater, dining for 400, and smart systems that play music and light up your footsteps as you walk around?

___ **C.** Both of the above?

Check your scores... *

Ten fab, Bill-centric questions. Give yourself: **1** point for each **A**, **5** points for each **B**, **10** points for each **C**. How did you do?

100. That's ten dead-on **C**s for the maximum 100. That's what I got...But I always score at the top of the class! Bill-tastic!

60–99. Hey, you're getting there! You're ready for complete global software domination, brutally crushing competitors, wearing clothes from the Gap, and generally being a nice guy. Scores over 75 are serious Bill material, who could be called upon to stand in for the real Bill in the event of a crisis. Cool!

16–59. Still some way to go. In software terms, you're still at the level of VP, Strategic Marketing in Emerging Eastern European Markets. (I.e., selling Word for DOS in Poland.) Keep at it!

Less than 15. Two words describe your level of Bill-ness. Steve. Jobs. (And you probably like your clothes "really soft.") Random!

WHO'S WHO
in **BILL'S**
Little World

Adams, Ansel	Photographer. Couldn't do color stuff, apparently.
Al-Waleed bin Talal, Prince	A really, really, really rich Arab dude.
Allen, Paul	Cofounder of Microsoft and now a really, really rich guy. Who squanders it on fast cars, no-hope technology, and the Portland Trailblazers.
Amazon.com	Virtual bookstore.
Amelio, Gilbert	Crappy old Apple CEO.
Anderson, Gillian	Scully (or is it Mulder?) on the X-Files.
Andreessen, Marc	Netscape whiz-kid and technology guy. Not a bit like me.
Aniston, Jennifer	Major babe in *Friends*.

Ballmer, Steve

One of my key VPs, and also very rich guy. Bald, but nobody's perfect.

Barksdale, Jim

Netscape. 'Nuff said.

Barnes & Noble

Real bookstore.

Bartz, Carol

CEO of Autodesk in sunny San Rafael. Chick. 'Nuff said.

Blair, Tony

U.K. president—loves Windows! (Hates smoking!)

Borg, the

Star Trek baddies.

Brown, Helen Gurley

Way ancient editor chick of *Cosmopolitan* magazine. Fired, at last.

Brunei, Sultan of

Another really, really, really rich Arab dude.

Bueller, Ferris

Like me, a way cool guy with a way cute chick! Hero of cult movie *Ferris Bueller's Day Off*.

Buffett, Warren

My big buddy, and also very, very, very rich. Bridge player and part-time investor.

Burroughs, William

Drug-crazed, homosexual author. Shot his wife (missed the glass).

Carlston, Doug	Former Broderbund CEO.
Case, Steve	America Online (AOL) CEO. Leading on-line service (until MSN).
Cassidy, David	'70s pop star.
Clapton, Eric	'70s, '80s, '90s pop star. Has slept with nearly EVERY cute chick on the planet!
Clark, Jim	Netscape. Again.
Clinton, Bill	President and CEO (of America). Bill #2, as I call him.
Clinton, Chelsea	Presidential daughter. Blossoming nicely, I think…
Cook, Scott	CEO of Intuit, the Quicken (MS Money competitor) guys.
Coupland, Douglas	Wrote *Microserfs.* I hated it! Burn it!
Cowpland, Michael	CEO of Corel, the Corel-DRAW! people.
Crawford, Cindy	Babe!!!!
Cray, Seymour	Designer of (non–Windows compatible) supercomputers.

da Vinci, Leonardo Renaissance dude.

Dey, Susan Actress in *The Partridge Family* and (later) *L.A. Law*.

Dick, Philip K. Science fiction author.

Duchovny, David The other one in *The X-Files*.

Eastwood, Clint Actor. Do you feel lucky, punk?

Ellison, Larry CEO of Oracle Corporation with weird Japanese fixation, and obsession with beating ME!

Elvis The King.

Ferron, William Lawyer at Seed & Berry.

Feynman, Richard Richard Feynman, you're my hero...Great scientist, identified cause of *Challenger* explosion, Nobel Prize winner.

Flowers, Gennifer Famous for sleeping with Bill Clinton. ALLEGEDLY!

Forbes, Steve Rich *Forbes* magazine guy and failed presidential candidate.

Frankenberg, Bob Ex-Novell dude. Who cares?

French, Melinda
My darling wife, and mother of Baby Bill. Who says office romances don't work?

Gap, the
The only place to shop for clothes.

Gates, Bill
Me! I rule, OK!

Gates, Jennifer Katharine
My darling, first-born daughter (a.k.a Bill Jr. or Baby Bill). Kiss, kiss, snuggems. Sweet Baby Jennifer. I love that girl.

Gates, Kristi
My sister.

Gates, Libby
My other sister.

Gates, Mary
My mom.

Gates, William
My pop.

Gerstner, Louis
IBM. Oh, them.

Glaser, Rob
CEO of Progressive Networks, ex-Microsoft. Thinks I'm too abrasive. What does he know?

Gore, Al
Clinton's Veep. Stole my book!!!

Grisham, John
Author of absurdly popular legal-inspired fiction. Nontechnical.

Grove, Andrew

Head of Intel, the maker of all those processor chips for PCs. And author of *Only the Paranoid Survive.*

Hall, Jerry

Soon to be ex-Mrs. Mick Jagger?

Hawking, Stephen

Author of *A Brief History of Time* and famous genius spastic/scientist.

Hendrix, Jimi

Dead rock star, and Paul Allen OBSESSION.

Herbold, Bob

Microsoft COO. And STILL earns more than me!

Ho, Dr. David

AIDS reseacher and *Time* Man of the Year. Totally random!

Internet, the

It's so OBVIOUS! Duh!

Isaacson, Walter

Time editor who interviewed me.

Jackson, Michael

Singer, black(?). Accused of child molestation and large amounts of plastic surgery. (Previously famous for big-selling album *Thriller.*)

Jagger, Mick
Rolling Stones singer with big lips.

Jennings, Laura
Chick, Microsoft, content. Cute-ish.

Jobs, Steve
Apple founder, Pixar (*Toy Story*) founder. Industry golden boy. And TOTALLY undeserved!

Jones, Gwyn
Ex-CEO of Serif, the PagePlus (MS Publisher competitor) guys. Another loser!

Justice, Department of
A bunch of ***** with an irrational desire to get Microsoft.

Kaplan, Jerry
Of GO and PenPoint (pen-based OS) fame.

K, JF
John F. Kennedy. Famous dead president.

Kahn, Philippe
Ex-CEO of Borland (onetime big company) whose reach exceeded his grasp when he acquired AshtonTate. Now scrapes a living from Starfish Software.

Kasparov, Gary
Mediocre chess player. (Compared to me, that is.)

Katzenberg, Jeffrey   Ex-Disney, now member of the "Dream Team" of Katzenberg, Spielberg, Geffen. They haven't done anything yet, but I'm sure it's gonna be great.

Kensit, Patsy   Actress. Married Gallagher (Oasis) brother.

King, Martin Luther   Civil rights leader.

Kinsley, Michael   I recruited him to produce *Slate*, my Webzine. Hmmm.

Lee, Adelyn   Oracle ex-employee and center of Larry scandal.

Letterman, David   Cool talk show dude. Does Top Tens, I think, but not as good as mine...

Liam, Noel and   Gallagher brothers, Oasis. Of course!

Lightyear, Buzz   Space Ranger, hero of *Toy Story*.

Lola, Baby   Madonna's kid.

Love, Courtney   Mrs. Kurt Cobain and singer in Hole. Whoever they are.

Lucas, George   *Star Wars*. Coming again soon.

Madonna	Actress, singer, and mother of Baby Lola.
Mao, Chairman	Communist leader, China.
McCartney, Lennon and	The Beatles. Oasis "inspiration."
McCaw, Craig	McCaw Communications and Teledesic.
McNealy, Scott	Big boss (loser) at Sun.
Mechanics, Mike and the	Who?
Monroe, Marilyn	Dead actress, famous for singing Happy Birthday to JFK.
Morissette, Alanis	Canadian rock chick.
Murdoch, Rupert	Media Mogul. That's MY next job...
Myhrvold, Nathan	One of the big guys at Microsoft. Very technical. Coauthor of *The Road Ahead*. Likes the Talking Heads, but nobody's perfect.
Noel, Liam and	*See* Liam, Noel and.
Noorda, Ray	Ex-Novell, now Caldera. Went and cried all the way to the FTC.
Nostradamus	Visionary, like me. Forecast the success of DOS

and Windows and the coming of the Ultimate Dictator. Couldn't possibly be me!

Patterson, Tim
Wrote DOS. (Oops. Did I say that?)

Perot, Ross
A sad, strange little man who ran for president. And failed.

Perry, Matthew
Actor in *Friends*.

Polese, Kim
CEO of Marimba. Hot, smart Italian babe! Yeaaahhhh! (Just kidding about that Polecat stuff. And she runs a GREAT software company.)

Pope, the
Leader of another really, really big corporation.

President, Amateur Gynecology Club
Some disgraced Microsoft exec, center of a sexual harassment e-mail scandal.

President, American
Bill #2. *See* Clinton, Bill...

President, Microsoft Corp.
Me! *See* Gates, Bill...

Raikes, Jeff
Yet another Microsoft guy.

Reiser, Paul
Star of *Mad About You*; author of *Couplehood*.

Reno, Janet	Justice Department chick. Get off my case, OK?
Rinearson, Peter	Coauthor of *The Road Ahead*.
Road Ahead, The	My book. It's great. Buy it!
Romero, John	Too-cool games developer of Doom, Quake, and BFG (Big F***ing Gun) fame. He rocks! And he shares my birthday, too!
Rottweiler	It's a dog, apparently.
Schmidt, Eric	Ex-Sun, takes on Novell top job. Big mistake.
Schwimmer, David	Actor in *Friends*. Does Jennifer Aniston (on-screen only).
Secret, Victoria's	Sexy underwear. The models are always OK, too.
Seed & Berry	One of my many lawyers. Get that Secret Diary, guys!
Shakespeare, William	Dead English writer dude.
Silverberg, Brad	Another Microsoft guy. Important-ish. I think.
Simonyi, Charles	Microsoft star software developer, now past his

prime. Not Mexican—
that's just my little joke
at the expense of the
politically incorrect Word
Thesaurus.

Sinatra, Frank   Crooner.

Spice Girls, the   Chick group. Yeaaahhhh!

Spielberg, Steven   Filmmaker extraordinaire.
                            Jaws, ET, Indiana Jones...

Stern, Howard   Awesome, supercool
                            "shock jock" nearly as
                            famous as me! He rocks!

Stonesifer, Patty   Microsoft chick. Broke
                            the glass ceiling...

Streep, Meryl   Actress.

Thatcher, Margaret   Ex-president (England)
                            and original Spice Girl,
                            apparently.

Travolta, John   Actor and Sweat Hog. I
                            can dance better! Just
                            joking about *The Catcher
                            in the Rye*.

Trebek, Alex   What is *Jeopardy*? I'll
                            take quiz shows for a
                            thousand, Alex.

Vader, Darth

Dark Lord and ruthless *Star Wars* antihero. Any resemblance to me is purely accidental. Besides, IMHO he's a big softy.

Waller, Robert James

Author of really mushy books.

Warhol, Andy

Dead celebrity, famous for just fifteen minutes. My diary's better than his!

Wars, Star

Allegorical tale of Good vs. Evil in the software biz.

Winblad, Ann

Venture capitalist and my "special friend" before I dumped her for Melinda.

Winer, Dave

Hmmm…Rich, nerd, Internet celebrity?

Wrigley's gum dude

No names, no embarrassment. Melinda's ex-boyfriend and heir to a small chewing gum fortune. Way short of $40 billion. Ha!

SELECTED
BIBLIOGRAPHY

► **By reading** my awesome Diary, you've demonstrated that you aspire to a higher level of "Bill-ness" than the average person. Cool! So check out my Top Twenty books about me and the fascinating industry that is the computer biz (and some of my favorite light reading)...

1. *The Road Ahead,* Bill Gates (with minor contributions from Nathan Myhrvold and Peter Rinearson)—is an all-time classic, and #1 on my recommended list. Buy it!

2. *Hard Drive,* James Wallace and Jim Erickson—is all about me.

3. *Overdrive,* James Wallace—the sequel, with even more about me.

4. *The Microsoft Way,* Randall Stross—He loves me! Yeaahhhh!

5. *I Sing the Body Electronic,* Fred Moody—a year at Microsoft (my awesome company).

6. *Deeper,* John Seabrook.

7. *Only the Paranoid Survive,* Andrew Grove.

8. *Startup,* Jerry Kaplan—the story of GO and how we (allegedly!) copied all their technology for Pen Windows.

9. *Microserfs,* Douglas Coupland—a novel, sort of about me.

10. *The Soul of a New Machine,* Tracy Kidder.

11. *The Highwaymen,* Ken Auletta—showing Nicholas the way by repurposing his *New Yorker* essays.

12. *Being Digital,* Nicholas Negroponte—profitably repurposing his *Wired* essays.

13. *Silicon Snake Oil,* Clifford Stoll—a contrarian view of technology.

14. *Accidental Empires: How the Boys of Silicon Valley Make Their Millions, Battle Foreign Competition and Still Can't Get a Date,* Robert X. Cringely—great title, but still WAY outsold by my own *Road Ahead.*

15. *The Molecular Biology of the Gene,* James D. Watson—is totally fascinating.

16. *Feynman's Lost Lecture: The Motion of Planets Around the Sun,* David Goodstein, Judith Goodstein, Richard Feynman.

17. *The Great Gatsby,* F. Scott Fitzgerald—should be *The Great Gatesby!*

18. *The Catcher in the Rye,* J. D. Salinger—is my all-time favorite (fiction that is) book.

19. *The Bridges of Madison County,* Robert James Waller—is pretty close, though!

20. The **Dilbert** books, Scott Adams—Yikes! This IS Microsoft!